Ethos and Education
in Ireland

Irish Studies

Robert Mahony
General Editor

Vol. 7

PETER LANG
New York • Washington, D.C./Baltimore • Bern
Frankfurt am Main • Berlin • Brussels • Vienna • Oxford

James Norman

Ethos and Education In Ireland

PETER LANG
New York • Washington, D.C./Baltimore • Bern
Frankfurt am Main • Berlin • Brussels • Vienna • Oxford

Library of Congress Cataloging-in-Publication Data

Norman, James.
Ethos and education in Ireland / James Norman.
p. cm. — (Irish studies; v. 7)
Includes bibliographical references and index.
1. Catholic schools—Ireland. 2. School environment—Ireland.
I. Title. II. Irish studies (New York, N.Y.); v. 7.
LC506.I73 N67   371.071'2417—dc21   2002023802
ISBN 0-8204-5728-0
ISSN 1043-5743

Die Deutsche Bibliothek-CIP-Einheitsaufnahme

Norman, James:
Ethos and education in Ireland / James Norman.
–New York; Washington, D.C./Baltimore; Bern;
Frankfurt am Main; Berlin; Brussels; Vienna; Oxford: Lang.
(Irish studies; Vol. 7)
ISBN 0-8204-5728-0

The paper in this book meets the guidelines for permanence and durability
of the Committee on Production Guidelines for Book Longevity
of the Council of Library Resources.

© 2003 Peter Lang Publishing, Inc., New York
275 Seventh Avenue, 28th Floor, New York, NY 10001
www.peterlangusa.com

Printed in the United States of America

Dedicated to my mother,
Florence O'Higgins-Norman

Contents

Foreword

AS a philosopher of education, I welcome the addition of this volume to Peter Lang's series on Irish Studies and find it gratifying that the publishers are extending their output in this area. After all, the curriculum is the one of the most obvious arenas through which a nation's culture is given expression and communicated to the young generation. The curriculum can prompt controversy regarding the very definition of Irishness. One area where issues of identity are very much to the fore concerns the place of the Irish language in schools. Must one speak Irish to be truly Irish? Is it realistic to expect the learning of Irish in school to lead to a revival of the language? Critical debate on the relationship between knowledge of the Irish language and Irish identity and on the project of reviving Irish through the classroom is rare. What discussion there is usually concerns only the effectiveness of different teaching methods. Anecdotal evidence suggests that significant numbers of young people seem to have opted out in spirit from Irish class. But this has not led to a critical inquiry into the status of compulsory Irish in the school curriculum.

There is also a paucity of studies dealing with religion, that other important element in Irish identity, and the role of schooling in supporting this identity. For example, the issue of the relationship between religion and the secular curriculum came to the fore in 1990s. In Ireland parents have the constitutional right to withdraw their children from religious education in the formative sense but it was hard to see how such withdrawal could be complete or absolute in practice because the rules of the Department of Education required the maintenance of a religious ethos in all primary schools. An essential element of the ethos was a mandatory relationship between religion and other subjects through the integrated curriculum. The assumption underlying this aspect of curriculum policy was that being religious was part of being Irish. The initiative on the issue was actually taken by the State and the revised document on the primary school curriculum changes the State's policy in the area.[1] The document affirms the significance for most Irish people of a religious perspective on life but it does not commit the State to a direct endorsement of the Christian view of human destiny. It is therefore no longer State policy to insist that the curriculum to endorse a single worldview. Elsewhere I have drawn attention to the disappointing lack of treatment of this issue in the educational literature.[2]

In this perspective, James Norman's book is a welcome contribution to the contemporary literature on the relationship between religion and schooling in Ireland. In spite of the State's withdrawal from direct endorsement of a religious world view, the vast majority of schools are religious and a religious ethos is the default ethos in most Irish schools. In the USA, Australia, the UK or in many European countries, Catholic schooling does not enjoy the same profile in educational and cultural life. James Norman's book examines how the confessional ethos of Irish schools fits into the Ireland of the twentieth-first century. The volume invites us to consider this question by examining how schools animated by a Catholic ethos in Ireland are managing to care for the welfare of their pupils.

Note, however, that every school is animated by a conception of the welfare of children. This applies even to schools that concern themselves solely and exclusively with the achievement of examination results. Individual schools and school systems will have different ideas of the remit of their duty for this welfare. Observing the education of his two children, British novelist, Tim Parks, has written with some bewilderment at what he perceives as the very different remit of the Italian school from that of its English counterpart.

For school offers no games, no extracurricular activities. There are no music lessons, no singing lessons, no school choir…no hockey, no cricket, no netball, no basketball, no football, no swimming, no athletics, no sports day, no school teams.[3]

Most of all what strikes him as the absence of any attempt to induce a family atmosphere in the school.

The school doesn't, as it does in England, pretend to offer a community that might in any way supplant the family, or rival Mamma. That's important. It doesn't, and later on the university won't either, try to create in the child the impression of belonging to a large social unit with its own identity. There is no assembly in the morning, no hymn singing, no prayers, no speech day…[4]

For his two children of six and eight, school is 'no more and no less than reading and writing and mathematics' and other school subjects.[5] Somewhat ironically, though, in spite of the attenuated and circumscribed or thin conception of the school's remit, religion is also part of the curriculum.

Irish and British schools are usually grounded in a wider or thicker conception of children's welfare. The school is perceived as an extension of the home in terms of providing personal support and overall care for young people. This conception of the school is most conspicuous in the case of boarding schools. Here is Irish novelist, Monk Gibbon's, description of the school in England that features in his novel, *The Pupil*. 'A school should be a large family –a small nation' is the slogan of the principal.[6] The narrator experiences it as a 'kind of miniature Plato's Republic', a 'cultured oasis', animated by the conviction 'that character is everything, and that everything without character is nothing'.[7]

Here is another account of the role of the school shared by committed teachers in many schools in the English-speaking world. Gervase Phinn, a school inspector, arrives in a boys' school in an area of disadvantage catering for children who have failed to get places in the traditional, academic secondary school. By virtue of attending this school the boys are already 'deemed to be failures' and arrive 'under-confident, with low self-esteem'.[8] The task of the school, explains the principal, is, 'first and foremost'…

to build up their confidence and self-esteem, continue to have high expectations for them and be sure they know, give them maximum support and
encouragement, develop their social skills and qualities of character to
enable them to enter the world feeling good about themselves...so they
develop into well-rounded young people with courage, tolerance, strong
convictions, lively enquiring minds and a sense of humour...I do really
believe...that those of us in education can really make a difference, particularly in the lives of less fortunate children, those who are labelled failures'.[9]

He tries, he says, to make the school 'like the good home that I
was brought up in, a place where there is work and laughter, hon-
esty and fairness'.[10] The image of home assumes even greater
salience in the Catholic school.

Traditionally schools in Ireland are perceived both as comple-
menting the work of the home in terms of religious or catechetical
formation as well as extending the parents remit of caring. The
school and its teachers stand *in loco parentis*. A moving incident of
which I was a witness communicates very well what this can mean
in practice. In a school that I was visiting, which was attached to a
convent, I was told that the police were searching for the body
of a parent who had died tragically. There was a great sense
of foreboding and sadness on the day of my visit and it came as a
relief when the body was recovered. I learned that the religious of
the community who owned the school had been helping to look
after the family over the weekend. This is the kind of service that
Catholic educators have given so generously and of which the
Church is rightly proud. It is an expression of the school as a locus
through which a religious vocation of total service can be given
expression. In this sense, the Catholic school can be defined by its
ethic of service.

There are two pillars of the Catholic ethic of service: the first is
one of service to the whole welfare of the child and the second is a
concern to ensure this welfare beyond the years of schooling. For
example, two keynote papers delivered at a large conference on
Catholic education held in Dublin in 2002 had the following two
titles that capture this remit very well: 'Catholic Schools as
Communities of Service: The US Experience' (by Joseph O'Keefe)
and 'Education for Life: The Heart of Catholic Education' (by
Thomas Groome). Of course, it can also be said of the Catholic
school that its concern for the welfare of children extends even

beyond adult life. The Catholic school, it can indeed be said, 'exists for purposes of soul'[11] in the sense of having a concern for the destiny of the human soul, although this aspect of its remit does not tend to be highlighted in the literature.

To what extent is it possible for Catholic schools to continue to offer the service to which it aspires? Certainly it is far more difficult in the light of declining numbers of religious in education. How can the wonderful aspects of this tradition of service be maintained in the twenty-first century?

Here I wish to draw attention to two professional strands of the school's undertaking to care for pupils. In both dimensions of this undertaking, caring is a part of trying to educate; it is not an activity in itself. The first is to ensure that the pupils learn. It is part of every teacher's job definition to care about this. To be sure, failure to succeed in learning may be due to factors beyond the control of the teacher – for example, domestic disharmony or illness. But teachers' primary responsibility is to try to teach their subject. In some cases, where the resistance of the pupils to school and to learning seems insurmountable, this may prove impossible. But it is simply not good enough to forgo the attempt to teach on the grounds that all efforts are doomed to failure unless we change the whole educational system or indeed the whole socio-economic system. Fashionable theories about re-defining what counts as intelligence may well be sustainable but they are not an excuse for giving up on trying to teach that constituency of the young population described as low achievers. The principal referred to previously invokes no high-faluting phrases about the 'failure of the system', 'narrow conception of intelligence' or the need for 'critical theory'.

The second strand refers to professional interventions aimed at helping students to cope with personal problems. In Ireland, these interventions come within the remit of guidance counsellor and/or chaplain, although not all schools have access to their services. Only in Community Schools does the chaplain enjoy a state salary and freedom from teaching duties. In attributing to counsellors/chaplains a professional role is this area is not to absolve the classroom teacher of responsibility. The demands of a teaching timetable do not normally permit teachers to provide the kind of one to one support that is often required. Yet, as a wise and experienced teacher, turned counsellor, observed to me the expression of sympathy and concern is not the exclusive prerogative of the professional. In cases where a teacher knows of some troubling domestic situation, what is needed at times may be a brief sympathetic word communicating awareness of the young person's situation and the stress she must be undergoing.

Yet situations arise that are beyond the competence of either teacher of guidance counsellor. For this reason I am impressed by this concluding chapter on the role of the chaplain. Rather than taking refuge in high theories about the 'whole person', the 'disadvantaged' and the usual generalities of aspirational rhetoric about the need to change attitudes, James Norman makes this practical proposal. He shows how the extension and formalisation of the role of the chaplain in all schools can assist schools bearing witness to the gospel. The personal witness and support provided by a specialised chaplain in all schools would be more telling that the best theories.

Dr. Kevin Williams,
Head of Education,
Mater Dei Institute of Education,
Dublin City University

Notes

1. See Department of Education and Science, *The Primary Curriculum: Introduction* (Dublin, The Stationery Office, 1999). For a discussion of this issue see also Williams, K. 'Faith and the Nation: Education and Religious Identity in the Republic of Ireland', *British Journal of Educational Studies*, vol. 47. no. 4 (December, 1999), pp. 317–31.
2. In Williams, K. and McNamara, G., 'The Landscape of Curriculum Inquiry in Ireland', in W. Pinar, ed, *Handbook of International Curriculum Inquiry* (Mahwah, New Jersey, Lawrence Erlbaum, forthcoming).
3. Parks, T. *An Italian Education* (London, Vintage, 2000), p. 287.
4. *Ibid.*
5. *Ibid.*
6. Gibbon, M., *The Pupil* (Dublin, Wolfhound Press, 1981), p. 14.
7. *Ibid.*, pp. 21, 75–6.
8. Phinn, G., *Over Hill and Dale* (London, Penguin, 2000), p. 152.
9. *Ibid.*, pp. 152–3, 171.
10. *Ibid.*, p. 171.
11. Gibbon, *The Pupil*, p. 76.

Acknowledgments

IN writing this book I received and benefited greatly from the advice, help and support of many people.

A special word of appreciation is due to my thesis supervisor Dr. Pádraig Hogan, Lecturer at the National University of Ireland, Maynooth and the other members of the Education Department at Maynooth, especially Professor John Coolahan, Dr. Maeve Martin, Senior Lecturer and Dr. Sheelagh Drudy, now Professor of Education at UCD.

I would also like to thank my colleagues at the Mater Dei Institute of Education for their support and advice, especially Dr. Kevin Williams, Head of Education.

Apart from the hours and days spent sitting in front of the PC, there were many hours of talking and probably boring my family and friends in conversations about ethos, education and pastoral care. I wish to thank all those who supported me through these conversations or with a kind word of encouragement especially, Paul, Frances, Ciarán, Derek, Peter, Fintan, Terry, Chris, Ed, Nancy, Paddy, Jennie and PJ.

Introduction

AS we begin the third millennium, the Catholic Church can reflect on an involvement in education that spans most of the last two thousand years. In Ireland the Church has been involved in education at least since the Celtic monasteries of the 5th century. These monastic schools taught a curriculum that combined formal religious studies such as scripture and theology with a range of classical disciplines such as Greek and Latin language and literature. The Christian or Catholic school thus had a dual motivation from its outset in that it was educational both in the catechetical and academic sense.

Since the nineteenth century the Catholic school in Ireland as we have come to know it has been managed by a local patron or trustee in the form of a bishop or religious community. For the most part, while the control and management of Irish Catholic schools have remained the same to today, Irish society is rapidly changing. As Irish society becomes more pluralistic and less homogeneous, there is a need for the trustees of Catholic schools to return to the roots of Catholic schooling in terms of its holistic aims and begin to channel their involvement in education to suit the needs of society today and to meet the demands of their original trust in terms of providing education to meet the needs of the poor.

In this book I explore the habitual nature of ethos in the Irish school through a reflection on the writings of Aristotle and Plato and the documents on education that have been produced by the Catholic Church over the last thirty-five years. I then compare the educational vision of these documents with the submissions of the Irish Bishops' Conference and the Conference of Religious of Ireland to the National Education Convention in Dublin in 1993.

Furthermore, I outline the combined findings of research into the ethos of Irish schools, which reveals a picture of operational ethos that values academic achievement, above all other dimensions of the human person. In this volume, research into the ethos of Irish Catholic schools is compared with research into the ethos of a Community school. The findings of this research suggest that many of the characteristics of the Catholic school, such as openness, a concern for the poor and a concern for the common good, are very prominent in the Community school. They also suggest that parents and students may be choosing the Catholic voluntary schools for reasons of their academic excellence rather than for religious formation or pastoral care.

For those who manage Catholic schools it is clear that religious trustees will have to engage in a period of deep reflection as to the best way to educate parents and teachers in the philosophy of Catholic schooling. Through a process of dialogue trustees can begin to move away from a solely academic focus to a more holistic and pastoral ethos in the Catholic school.

James Norman,
Mater Dei Institute of Education,
Dublin City University, Ireland
January 2003

Chapter 1

Ethos and Education

School ethos is the atmosphere that emerges from the interaction of a number of aspects of school life including teaching and learning, management and leadership, the use of images and symbols, rituals and practices, as well as goals and expectations.

A SIGNIFICANT part of the education debate in Ireland since the early 1990s has been taken up by various denominational and other groups seeking to articulate their values and goals in education. In this context the phrase 'school ethos' has been used to describe the particular character of many Irish schools. However, this is a phrase that means many things to many people and to a large extent has been misunderstood, partly due to the elusive nature of this concept.

Defining Ethos

The word *ethos* comes from the Greek word meaning habit. In its origins ethos has something to do with the development of a person's character, that is, an atmosphere where a person's values or moral habits are formed. A closer look at the word itself as used by Aristotle suggests that ethos implies the prevalent tone or sentiment of a community, the genius of an institution or system.[1] Consequently, the ethos of a school has to do with its tone and character, the intangible genius or spirit that permeates its endeavours giving a certain moral shape to all of its activities.

However, the ethos of a school is an elusive entity, the result of many influencing factors at work in the school community. School ethos is the atmosphere that emerges from the interaction of a number of aspects of school life, including teaching and learning, management and leadership, the use of images and symbols, rituals and practices, as well as goals and expectations. Regarding a school's goals, it is possible to distinguish between three different types of goals, instrumental, organisational and expressive. The instrumental goals refer to the transmission of academic learning, what is actually taught in the school's curriculum, while organisational goals have to do with the administration and structures that are put in place to facilitate that learning. However, the expressive goals have to do with the more intangible aspects of the school's outcomes such as its cultural activities, the formation of character, the cultivation of attitudes and the transmission of values. While the expressive goals are often a source of cohesion and unity within a school, these can be displaced by the instrumental goals, particularly in an exam-dominated education system such as we have at secondary school level in Ireland. This can cause the alienation of those students who are only weakly involved in the instrumental order, resulting in the development of their own student-based and anti-social expressive order.[2]

The challenge for schools is to be creative in finding ways to engage all students in the instrumental, organisational and expressive orders of the school. Recent developments in the second-level curriculum such as the Leaving Certificate (Applied) Programme, which offers an alternative to the traditional and more academic terminal examination, have helped many potential early school leavers to play a fuller role in the instrumental order of the school and consequently to complete their second-level education. The organisational order of Irish post-primary schools still relies heavily on a hierarchy with trustees and teachers at the top and students and parents lower down. There has been some progress in the development of student councils in many second level schools, although to date there is still no legal obligation requiring student representation on school boards of management. A school's mission statement will provide a good indication of the school's expressive goals. However, these goals can be displaced somewhat by the curriculum and organisational structures in the school, resulting in an expressive order which is in reality something significantly different to that which is contained in the mission statement. Consequently, it is clear that there can be counter forces at work, and that the school ethos at any given time is the outcome of a number of influences, instrumental, organisational and expressive, some of which will be reinforcing one another while others may be destructive and interfering.

For Aristotle ethos had to do with the development of goodness or character. In Book II of his *Ethics*, Aristotle draws out the habitual nature of character or ethos.

> Goodness is not produced in us either by nature or in opposition to nature; we are naturally capable of receiving it, and we attain our full development by habituation.[3]

In this sense then, the ethos of an institution such as a school is not something that can be taught or imposed, but rather it will arise from the dynamic life of the people involved in the institution. Aristotle goes on in Book II of his *Ethics* to explain how this habit will be influenced by the ordinary dealings that people have with their associates or colleagues. He emphasises that good moral development is the result of the interactions of good people with other good people. In this case goodness is not something that can be forced upon a person but it will arise from within the process of interactions between those involved. What is significant here is that ethos in the Aristotelian sense inheres in an institution in the same way that air fills a room, naturally and without direction or imposition. Ethos is an essential and implicit entity; it is unavoidable and cannot be separated from the school.

Anyone who has worked in or visited more than one school will have noticed the way in which each school has its own personality or character. I know of two school principals who were close friends and colleagues. One was appointed principal sometime after the first in a newly built school. He naturally turned to his friend for advice, which resulted in the second school having the same curriculum, the same organisational structures and the same colour uniform as the first school. However, despite these similarities each school still had its own distinctive character. When we compare one school with another, there is an essential difference, but what exactly is it that we perceive to have changed? We can observe that one school may have an emphasis on sports while another stresses music. Furthermore a school may contain quite a few denominational images and there may be a particular place of worship within the building. However, if we follow the Aristotelian understanding of ethos as something that arises habitually, this difference between schools has more to do with the process of inter-actions between staff, students, parents and management than it has to do with the instrumental or organisational dimensions of the school. For example, is the staff room a place where visitors and new teachers are made to feel welcome or are they assigned seats at the bottom of the lunch table? Is there an easy and open professional relationship between teachers and students or is it one based on hierarchy and control? Are teachers' relationships with ancillary staff such as cleaners, secretaries and caretakers based on parity or is there a residue of resentment among the latter resulting from a perceived lack of respect? Consequently, in the Aristotelian sense, school ethos is something that arises spontaneously from natural habit. It is the ordinary dealings that people have with each other and the manner in which they are carried out. A school's ethos can ultimately be described as the dominant pervading spirit or character of the institution resulting from the habits of behaviour of those who are part of it.[4]

In his *Politics* Aristotle refines his argument that ethos is the dominant spirit of a place or institution:

For the maintenance of any constitution, like its first establishment, is due, as a rule to the presence of the spirit or character proper to that constitution. The establishment and maintenance of democracy is due to the presence of a democratic spirit...the better the spirit, the better the constitution it gives rise to.[5]

Clearly then, the maintenance of a particular type of school is dependent upon the presence of a spirit or character proper to that type of school. If the spirit of a Christian school is absent or weak it will result in the school being something other than a Christian school. This highlights the need for a particular commitment on the part of all those involved in a school in order to achieve its goals. However, this raises the question, how does one achieve the appropriate spirit within a particular school and is it possible to achieve it without compromising the dynamic nature of the schools' ethos.

In *The Republic* Plato articulates the role of educators as guardians, arguing in favour of protecting youth from negative influences that they might encounter during their education. He even goes as far as condoning the use of censorship by the guardians in order to achieve the desired ethos.[6] Plato had a paternalistic vision of ethos in that he saw the development of character primarily in terms of the implementation of precept and the compliance of those concerned. On the other hand, Aristotle claimed that after a preliminary education it is through 'habituation' that this spirit or ethos will be achieved.[7]

However, it requires more than just a preliminary education to ensure that, for example, society remains democratic. There is a need for society constantly to revisit and reassess its democratic goals, working them out in the light of particular situations as they arise. Consequently, many forums such as media, universities and associations are required so that society can continue to educate itself in the midst of its habitual life. In other words, there is a need to develop a culture that is both self-reflective and habitual. Similarly in a school, it would be necessary for the ethos, that is, the pervading atmosphere, to be nourished by a healthy dialogue so as to inform and give vision to the life of the institution. This can be provided through ongoing staff in-service training and by all those involved engaging in a process of critical reflection concerned with fundamental issues affecting the goals of the school. The working out of the school's statements on bullying, equality and Relationships Sexuality Education provide an opportunity for staff, parents, management and students to enter into a dialogue and to recharge the school's spirit or habitual ethos. However, this requires that school management be willing to allow a free dialogue and reflection on these issues and that they do not seek to direct or impose their own concerns onto the staff, students and parents.

Dialogue in this sense does not refer to the skill of sorting out a problem or misunderstanding. As well as considering other positions, dialogue also seeks to listen to tradition and asks in what way the wisdom of tradition can throw light on the circumstances of the present. In so far as dialogue is a disposition it is as Pádraig Hogan explains *'what we are'* and involves a *'willingness to put the claim to truth in one's own perspective at risk, in the effort to achieve a more inclusive understanding'*.[8] In a school it is the teacher who will be the principal agent for promoting a disposition of dialogue. The manner of a teacher's response in an interpersonal exchange with students influences directly the ethos of the school. To rush in with a set of ready-made answers or codes of behaviour will contribute to the development of a culture of resentment among the students and create an ethos that relies on compliance rather than dialogue and critical reflection. The disposition of dialogue assists in the emergence of the student's personal identity in his or her encounters with tradition, others and human experience. Consequently, commitment to school ethos is high as each person has been allowed personally to encounter and make new the tradition out of which the school has come.

Ethos and the Catholic School

From its beginning the Catholic Church has been involved in education as a consequence of the teaching mission it believes it has received from its founder, Jesus Christ.[9]

> Go therefore and make disciples of all nations, baptising them in the name
> of the Father and of the Son and of the Holy Spirit, teaching them to observe
> all that I have commanded you.
>
> (Matthew 28:18)

Like Aristotle, Jesus saw goodness or character as something that was achieved through the habitual relationship of a people with each other and God. Previous to Jesus, the Jewish Pharisees had formulated a code of behaviour that was aimed at developing goodness.[10] However, this code had become rigid and dead and unable to explain the ordinary situations of people's lives such as sickness and poverty. In this sense, the Pharisees had developed a custodial sense of ethos where adherence to the code was of primary importance. On the other hand Jesus taught an internal goodness of the heart over goodness based on compliance to externals.[11] In the Gospels, people's commitment to the teachings of Jesus arises out of their companionship with him.[12] In 1979, the Catholic Church issued a document, which was concerned with its catechetical or teaching mission. *Catechesi Tradendae* declared that Jesus taught through his life as a whole:

> ...his teaching can only be explained by the fact of his words, his parables
> and his arguments are never separable from his life and his very being.
> Accordingly, the whole of Christ's life was a continual teaching: his
> silences, his miracles, his gestures, his prayer, his love for his people, his
> special affection for the little and the poor.[13]

The ethos of dialogue is central to the Gospel in which Jesus invites those who follow him into a more complete relationship with the Jewish tradition while acknowledging their freedom to reject this relationship.[14]

An examination of the educational documents of the Catholic Church since the Second Vatican Council (1963-6) reveals a return to an understanding of ethos that is concerned with dialogue and the integration of faith, culture and life. The first document of importance on education to proceed from the Second Vatican Council was the *Declaration on Christian Education* (1965), which placed the dignity of the human person at the centre of the Church's educational mission. Here the Church articulates its belief that the aim of education is to develop harmoniously students' physical, moral and intellectual qualities, helping them to devote themselves willingly to the promotion of the common good.[15] In other words, in an Aristotelian sense, the Church believes that education has to do with the development of a person's character.[16] The document goes on to expand on how goodness of character can be achieved through a partnership of parents, teachers and the state. While the document teaches the importance of introducing young people to the tradition and heritage of previous generations it also articulates the belief that young people should be provided with the opportunity to understand and respect those of other cultures and faiths. The document goes on then to warn governments against allowing a situation to arise by which any group would achieve a monopoly in education that would detract many from the rights of parents and would be inconsistent with the pluralism that exists in may societies.[17] In essence the Declaration on Christian Education reflects openness in the Church concerning education and a belief that education has to do with the development of the whole person, promoted by an integration of faith, culture and life.

The next major document from the Catholic Church concerning education was *The Catholic School* (1977), which identified the school's purpose with the wider mission of the Church. Once again this mission is articulated as having to do with the development of a person's character:

> The Catholic school is committed to the development of the whole man, since in Christ, the Perfect Man, all human values find their fulfilment and unity.[18]

Once again we find that the Church's teaching on education concurs with the Aristotelian understanding of ethos in that both are concerned with the development of character. In this document the Church claims that the development of the whole person is achieved through a 'synthesis of culture and faith'. Implied in this statement is the understanding that in order for a person's character to be developed they must enter into a dialogue involving faith, life and culture. The Catholic school is seen as a place where this dialogue can take place and where young people can be helped to achieve a harmony in their lives. In a clear rejection of a paternalistic concept of ethos, the document disavows the use of the Catholic school as a place for 'so called proselytism' or 'imparting a one sided outlook' or where a 'pre-cast conclusions' are offered to students.[19] The document envisaged the ethos of the Catholic school as an atmosphere where young people will not only be allowed to question but also will be trained and encouraged to reflect critically upon their faith and culture so as to develop as people of character.

In the 1988 document *The Religious Dimension of Education in a Catholic School (RDECS)*, the Church strongly asserts its right to establish schools, as based upon the right to freedom of conscience.

It claimed that not to be allowed this freedom would be a denial of religious freedom.[20] However, it tempers this claim by acknowledging its duty not to become involved with the indoctrination of youth saying that:

> To proclaim or to offer is not to impose…the latter suggests a moral violence which is strictly forbidden, both by the Gospel and by Church law.[21]

Here the Church once again makes a clear statement about the education of the young, rejecting anything that might detract from their fundamental freedom, which is necessary for the development of character. In the same document the Church considers the religious dimension of school climate and culture, examining the way these impact upon young people. The Church highlights the need to develop an ethos in the school that will help young persons achieve a balance in their life where faith and culture are concerned:

> …the world of human culture and the world of religion are not like two parallel lines that never meet; points of contact are established within the human person.[22]

Consequently, in a Catholic school the Church sees the development of the person as the responsibility of the whole school and not just of those qualified in the role of the religious education teacher. In essence this document seeks to highlight an integration of all aspects of the curriculum in order to bring about an integration of faith and culture in the student's life. As in previous documents the tone here is one of openness and dialogue.[23] While acknowledging the importance of the religious education programme in dealing with the various questions that arise for young people,[24] the Church warns against its dominance at the cost of the autonomy of other subjects.[25] In other words, this document views the ethos of the Catholic school as the atmosphere that arises from an open dialogue between faith, science, culture and ecology in order to achieve a balance in the development of the student's character. This emphasis on a balanced or well-rounded character concurs with the Aristotelian understanding of ethos and education.[26] In essence this document sees the habitual life of the school as the primary means of achieving an ethos that encourages an integration of faith, life and culture, ultimately resulting in the development of the student's character.

The most recent major Catholic document on education, *The Catholic School on the Threshold of the Third Millennium* (1998) continues many of the themes of its predecessors. Once again, it identifies the 'synthesis between faith and culture' as a distinguishing characteristic of the Catholic school. However, it goes on to develop the importance of what it calls the 'educating community' in the Catholic school. This document describes the Catholic school's ethos as constituted by the interactions of those who make up the school community, naming in particular the students, parents, teachers, administrators and on-teaching staff.[27] In an Aristotelian sense, the document highlights the importance of the habitual nature of the ethos in a Catholic school. Consequently, the Church attaches a particular significance to the quality of the relationships that contribute to the atmosphere in which the student's character is formed.

> ...a student needs to experience personal relations with outstanding educators, and what is taught has greater influence on the student's formation when placed in a context of personal involvement, genuine reciprocity, coherence of attitudes, lifestyles and day-to-day behaviour.[28]

The document concludes by placing the primary responsibility for creating the positive ethos of the school with the teachers, saying that it depends chiefly on them whether the Catholic school achieves its purposes.

In conclusion then, we can say that all of the Catholic Church's documents on education since the Second Vatican Council have had a common theme in relation to the ethos of Catholic schools. In identifying the habitual nature of school ethos and in placing the development of character at the heart of education these documents present some parallels with the Aristotelian vision of education as outlined in the *Ethics*. It is interesting to note how little these documents are concerned with the management or administration of schools as a means of maintaining ethos. The Church sees the school as sharing in her mission and places the full development of the human person at the centre of this mission. In each of the post-conciliar documents the Church stresses the open nature of its educational vision, encouraging students to dialogue with other cultures and faiths so as to understand themselves and others more fully. Ultimately, the Church desires that students in Catholic schools will be helped to integrate their faith and culture in such a way that they will become more whole as human beings. This integration will be achieved through the relationships of students with their teachers and all those involved in the Catholic school.

Ethos and the Irish Catholic School

An examination of the Irish Catholic Church's presentations to the National Education Convention in 1993 reveals a vision of ethos that is to some degree significantly different from that of the post-conciliar documents outlined above. In their submission the Irish Bishops initially outlined the aim of Christian education as being concerned with the development of the whole person.

> Education is designed to foster the growth of the person in every dimension–aesthetic, creative, critical, cultural, emotional, intellectual, moral, physical, social and spiritual.[29]

Clearly, this statement can be described as reflecting some of the dominant themes of the Vatican documents on education.

However, the Bishops then go on to describe their role in Platonic terms, claiming their right to act as guardians of the school's ethos:

> Such a right includes the general direction and government of the school, the ordering of religious instruction and worship and the appointment of teachers. For the State to insist on management structures which would inhibit the patrons/trustees in the exercise of their responsibility to guarantee the denominational and religious character of the school would mean...depriving the Catholic Community of its unambiguous right to determine the ethos and philosophy of their schools.[30]

The overall tone of the Bishops' submission is legalistic and paternalistic. Ultimately, the Bishops view the school in terms of the handing on of a tradition without any mention of developing a dialogue with the tradition and allowing the present school community to achieve a new 'synthesis' of faith, life and modern culture in the light of its tradition:

> A school will see may generations pass through its doors in its lifetime. The school is held in trust for successive generations of children of the Catholic community by the patron/trustee who is guarantor that the character of the school is assured into the future.[31]

The other major submission from the Catholic Church to the National Education Convention was made on behalf of the Conference of Religious of Ireland (CORI). While this document adopted a more conciliatory approach to the concept of dialogue in educational matters,[32] it also strongly rejected any attempt by the State to increase its influence over schools, claiming that this would inhibit the trustees' ability to maintain the original ethos of the schools. Speaking about the possibility of new devolved Local Education Committees, which had been suggested by the Government, CORI attempted to safeguard the autonomy of individual Boards of Management in relation to ethos:

> In some instances, for example, in relation to school ethos, it would be important that the new committees do not encroach on areas of responsibility and discretion currently vested in individual school boards.[33]

Furthermore, in relation to possible changes by Government to the structures of schools' Boards of Management, CORI rejected any structures that might take away from the rights of trustees to maintain a particular ethos in the school. It is for this reason that CORI:

> ...asserted the right of the trustee to determine the precise nature of school boards. (CORI) does not feel that the changes proposed in the composition of Boards of Management would give sufficient protection to the trustees with regard to school ethos and would not allow them to fulfil their responsibilities.[34]

Clearly then, we can see that CORI, like the Irish Bishops, presented to the National Education Convention a paternalistic understanding of ethos as it applies to schools. They perceived their role in terms of maintaining a tradition, which they had received in trust for future generations. Furthermore, in their submissions to the NEC, neither the Bishops nor CORI acknowledged the habitual nature of a school's ethos, which arises out of the interactions of those who make up the school community. Since the National Education Convention, neither the Bishops nor CORI have significantly altered their view that the Catholic ethos of the school is best served through trusteeship or the role of the patron. A recent presentation to a major conference concerned with school culture and ethos did reflect some change in the view of Religious trustees where ethos is concerned:

> ...there is a growing acceptance, among religious, of the view, expressed in the report of the National Education Convention (1994), that ethos is not something that can be 'determined' or 'handed on' to schools by trustees. Rather religious have embraced the understanding of ethos...(as) a dynamic feature of the whole school community.[35]

Despite this acknowledgement, the main view expressed by CORI at this conference was that they could best influence Catholic Schools and national educational policy through what they described as 'proactive trusteeship'. Consequently, we can say that to date CORI still rely on their role in management to influence the ethos of schools.

It seems that a gap has developed between the understanding of ethos as outlined in the Church's post-conciliar documents and as outlined in the presentations to the National Education Convention in 1993 and subsequent documents from the Irish Bishops and the Conference of Religious of Ireland. On the one hand, the Vatican documents articulate an understanding of ethos based on the need for dialogue of faith and culture, dealing with what actually goes on in a school. On the other hand, the Catholic trustees in Ireland see their role primarily in terms of maintaining an ethos which remains faithful to the trust that they have received from the founders of Catholic schools. In conclusion we can say that the Aristotelian understanding of ethos is concerned with the development of a person's character and the atmosphere in which this development will take place. In an Aristotelian sense, ethos can be described as the dominant or pervading tone or character of a place or institution. Unlike the paternalistic notion of ethos found in Plato's *Republic*, Aristotle's understanding sees ethos as arising from natural habit. Ethos is an elusive but intrinsic dimension to school life and is an outcome of many influencing factors, not least the ordinary manner in which people deal with each other. However, an important feature of this habitual concept of ethos is the development of a disposition of dialogue. This is a disciplined process in which the members of the school community place 'who they are' in dialogue with the tradition and other belief systems in order to achieve a synthesis of their faith, life and culture.

The Catholic Church's post-conciliar documents on education strongly concur with the Aristotelian concept of ethos, placing the development of the whole person at the centre of education. The Vatican documents present a model of schools that are open and inclusive, helping students to consider different cultures and faiths in the hope of achieving a better understanding of themselves and others. For the most part the Vatican documents promote an ethos in schools that encompasses collective attitudes, beliefs and values and this arises out of the relationships of staff, students and management. However, this vision of school ethos fails to be transferred to the Irish Church as revealed in the submissions to the National Education Convention and subsequent presentations. While both the Irish Bishops and CORI place the full development of the whole person at the centre of education, they fail to acknowledge in any significant way that this development is something which arises out of the habitual relationships in a school. The Vatican documents suggest that patrons/trustees cannot legislate for an ethos, it is something that can only be facilitated from within the life of the school. The trustees of Irish Catholic schools have adopted a paternalistic understanding of ethos, which can be said to have developed an attitude of compliance among those who work in Catholic schools. Consequently, teachers do not challenge the status quo in Catholic schools and are slow to bring themselves and their students into dialogue with the tradition of the school. This results in an ethos of compliance rather than commitment.

Notes

1. Aristotle's *Rhetoric* Book II, xii–xiv.
2. B. Bernstein., *Class, Codes and Control*, Volume II, (London, Routledge, 1975) p.139.
3. Aristotle, *Ethics, Book II, Section I*, in Burnett, J., *Aristotle on Education*, (Cambridge, University Press, 1967).
4. See K. Williams., *Understanding Ethos – A Philosophical and Literary Exploration in School Culture and Ethos, Cracking the Code*, (Dublin, Marino, 2000) p.74 for a fuller exploration of the phrase ethos.
5. Aristotle, *Politics, Book VIII, Section i*, in J. Burnett, *Aristotle on Education*, (Cambridge, University Press, 1967).
6. Plato's *Republic*, Book II, Section 377 b–c, in B. Jowett, *The Dialogues of Plato*, Vol. 4. p. 141
7. Aristotle, *Politics*, VIII, Section ii.
8. See P. Hogan., *The Custody and the Courtship of Experience*, (Dublin, Columba Press, 1995) p.136.
9. *Catechesi tradendae*, 1979, article 15.
10. Deut. 5:7–21.
11. Matthew 6: 4–6.
12. Mark 3:14
13. *Catechesi Tradendae*, 1979, article 9.
14. Mark 10:17–22.
15. Declaration on Christian Education, 1965, article 2.
16. *Ibid*. article 5.
17. *Ibid*. article 6.
18. *The Catholic School*, 1977, article 35.
19. *Ibid*. articles 19, 27.
20. *Religious Dimension of Education in a Christian School*, 1988, article 34.
21. *Ibid*. article 6.
22. *Ibid*. article 51.
23. *Ibid*. article 1.
24. *Ibid*. article 70.
25. *Ibid*. article 52.
26. *Ethics*, Book II.

27. *The Catholic School on the Threshold of the Third Millennium*, 1998, article 1.
28. *Ibid.*
29. National Education Convention, *Presentation of the Irish Bishops Conference*, (Dublin, 1993).
30. *Ibid.*
31. *Ibid.*
32. National Education Convention, *Presentation of the Conference of Religious in Ireland*, (Dublin, October, 1993) pp.3–5.
33. *Ibid.* p.10.
34. *Ibid.* p.12.
35. See T. McCormack, *Future Directions for Trusteeship, in School Culture & Ethos, Cracking the Code*, (Dublin, Marino, 2000) p.155.

Chapter 2

Custody of Irish Education

The statistics regarding the ownership and management of Irish primary and second-level schools reveal a rather homogeneous picture of the control and management of Irish education at the start of this millennium; a picture that can be described as mainly denominational and for the most part Catholic.

D URING the last decade of the twentieth century, the Irish Catholic Church fought hard to maintain its role as patron/trustee in Irish schools. Without this role the Irish Church saw no other way of maintaining the character of Irish Catholic schools. The Church's approach raises a number of questions about their participation in Irish education and how they carry out their role as patron/trustee in relation to the other partners in education.

Historical Background

Catholic schooling in modern times officially began in Ireland with the passing of the Relief Act in 1782 by the Irish Parliament of the day. This Act allowed Catholics to teach and conduct schools without fear of persecution. This came after a period of Penal Laws during which all ecclesiastical organisation was prohibited. By the nineteenth century, the struggle between the majority Catholic Church and the State for control of the national primary school system could be said to have been a struggle to mould the consciousness of the Irish people. On the one hand, the State sought to provide an education system through which the Irish people could be formed as good citizens of the British Empire. Initially the British Government pursued a policy of Anglicisation by operating constraints on the language and culture promoted in the schools. While on the other hand, the Catholic Church sought to educate people in the laws of the Church and to develop a loyalty to Rome and secondly to contribute towards a free Ireland in which Catholics could live by the laws of the Church without persecution. In fact, it is possible to trace the roots of the present paternalistic ethos in Irish schools back to that time and Catholic Church's response to the British Government's attempts to extend its influence in schools.

In 1831, the Government established the National School System, inviting existing denominational schools to join it. The aim of this system was to create multi-denominational schools where both Catholic and Protestant children would be educated together in literacy with religious instruction offered outside of school hours by their respective churches. There was some support for this move towards a more plural education system, even from within the churches themselves, as the famous James Doyle, Bishop of Kildare and Leighlin, pronounced:

> I do not know any measure which could prepare the way for better feeling in Ireland than uniting children at an early age, and bringing them up in the same school, leading them to commune with one another, and to form those little intimacies and friendships which often subsist through life.[1]

However, for the most part the Catholic Church in the nineteenth century did not support the mixing of students from different denominations. The subsequent appointment of Cardinal Paul Cullen to the Catholic See of Armagh in 1850 saw the consolidation of this stance on education, which for the most part rejected any school in which Catholic children could not receive instruction in their faith during school hours.

> If also at any time there be established schools in which the Parish Priest's rights are not recognised, or which he is not entitled to visit, let them take care that Catholic children do not frequent them.[2]

By the second half of the nineteenth century the Catholic Church had gained a strong and influential position in Irish society giving it the confidence to pursue its goal of denominational education. As most of the trustees of primary schools were representatives of the local church authorities, effectively the National School System became segregated on religious grounds. Furthermore, in 1859 the Catholic Church succeeded in winning the right to occupy fifty per cent of the seats on the Board of Commissioners for National Education.[3] The Catholic Church had been successful in establishing a denominational primary system. This meant that the Catholic Church was now in a position to create their own ethos in primary schools mainly through religious instruction and the role of the local clergy in the management of the schools.

The passage of the Intermediate Education Act in 1878 made government grants possible to assist secondary education. This act defined intermediate education as the stage of education between primary instruction, and professional or higher studies. This aid came in the form of payment by results, with grants being awarded in direct relation to success rates in intermediate examinations.[4] The 'payment by results' system in second-level schools meant that the Church was left to run schools as it saw fit. While it is true that the Church benefited from the lack of interference from the state, it is equally true that the state benefited from an education system, which was, for the most part, funded and run, by thousands of male and female religious for little or no cost to the state. After 1924 capitation grants were paid to second-level schools, as well as incremental salaries to teachers, although until quite recently the Church in the form of patron/trustee was responsible for teachers' basic salary. Since 1967, 90% of the capital expenditure and all operational costs in Catholic voluntary secondary schools have been paid by the state.[5]

Since 1999 the Irish Government has funded the total building of all new secondary schools. This means that the legal ownership of future schools will be in the hands of the State. However, the trusteeship of the Catholic schools will remain with the Bishops and the various Religious Orders, thus allowing them the ability to perpetuate their value system through the schools' ethos and personnel.

Once independence from the British was achieved in 1921, the *de facto* denominational nature of the Irish school system was quickly recognised by the new State and became institutionalised. The reason for this was two-fold. First, the Catholic Church had previously played an important role through its schools of helping to develop an Irish cultural nationalism; and secondly, the fledgling state with little resources was not about to take on the burden of running the entire education system. Thus, a previous informal association between Irish nationalism and Irish Catholicism became what has been described as a 'symbiotic' marriage whereby the new Irish State and the Catholic Church worked hand in hand to develop an Irish Catholic society where both Gaelic and Catholic values would be promoted especially through education.[6]

Ethos and School Management

As a consequence of the historical development of Irish education, the picture today is unique, in that the Catholic Church manages the majority of Irish schools in one form or another. At primary level, according to the 1997 Irish Government statistics, there are 3,193 ordinary primary schools in Ireland of which only 23 are multi-denominational and under the direct trusteeship of parents. The rest of the primary schools are denominational with 93% under the patronage of the Catholic Church. At the secondary school level, there are over 420 Catholic voluntary schools catering for more than 200,000 students, which accounts for 60% of the total school enrolment of this age group. Another 15% of students attend 86 Community/Comprehensive schools, in which for the most part the Catholic Diocese or Religious Orders act as co-trustees.

The remaining 25% of the post-primary student population attend the 246 vocational schools and community colleges, which while multi-denominational in theory, most commonly have a majority of Catholic students, parents, teachers and representation on their Boards of Management from the local Catholic Diocese.[7]

These statistics regarding the ownership and management of Irish primary and second-level schools reveal a rather homogeneous picture of the control and management of Irish education at the start of this millennium; a picture that can be described as mainly denominational and for the most part Catholic. These statistics endorse what I have already said concerning the Irish Catholic Church's concept of ethos and its desire to influence the character of schools through its managerial role. At no stage since 1831 has the official Church sought to promote or develop any other form of schooling except that over which it has complete or decisive influence. This has resulted in the Catholic Church achieving a lion's share over the control of Irish schooling. Even in the vocational/community college sector, which is the nearest thing in Ireland to a state school system, the official Church will usually have representation on the Boards of Management and will be involved in the selection of teachers. Clearly then apart from the 26 multi-denominational schools, every other type of school in Ireland will have some degree of influence in its management from the official Catholic Church.

Ethos and Choice in Education

It could be argued that the present situation regarding the Catholic Church's control and management of Irish schools is reflective of the traditionally homogeneous nature of Irish society. However, whatever about the past, Irish society today is increasingly more diverse and as with other western societies there have been many changes in how we see ourselves and the world we live in. Many of these changes can be summed up in the expression *post-modernism*, which describes our time, a time when the traditional culture based on the value of ultimate meaning in life has been replaced by a culture of convenience and consumerism. Boundaries have been pushed back and for many Irish people consumerism and self-need replace any abiding values of the spirit. Large shopping malls have been described as the 'new cathedrals' replacing the churches as the focus of our communities. In this context, it is not surprising that some Irish people are now demanding a choice in every aspect of their lives including religion and education. On the other hand the status quo regarding the Catholic Church's role in Irish education remains for the most part unchallenged. There are two reasons for this: first, the strength of the Church in the control and management of most Irish schools; and second, the weakness of student and parental influence in Irish education. This was illustrated recently at post-primary level when the views of both parents and students failed to influence the decision of striking teachers not to teach examination classes during the spring of 2001.

An implication of the homogeneous nature of Irish education is that children whose parents belong to a ethnic minority or whose religious affiliations are other than with the Catholic Church have found it particularly hard to realise the educational choice which they are guaranteed in the Irish Constitution which states that parents will not be forced to send their children to any particular type of school.[8] However, parents who are not Catholic often find themselves having to opt for the local Catholic school due to various restraints on their choice such as distance, inconvenience and finance, especially in rural and in less advantaged areas. Furthermore, due to the largely homogeneous nature of the student population in Irish schools, it can be hard to assess if non-catholic students in Catholic schools experience religious or racial intolerance. However, some recent research seems to suggest that there is some evidence of religious prejudice in Irish Catholic schools among the student population.[9] What is clear is that many of the parents who choose to send their children to multi-denominational schools do so because of the perceived absence of official Church control and the high degree of tolerance which is promoted in this sector.[10] While many children of ethnic minorities have had a good experience of Irish Catholic schools to date, between now and the year 2010, the high numbers of refugees and asylum seekers who have come to Ireland as well as the increase in migrants will force the Government and the Catholic Church to revisit the issue of pluralism in education. If all parents in Ireland are to have a real choice in education the Government will have to fund all schools equally, whether Catholic, Jewish, Muslim or multi-denominational. At the same time the Irish Church will have to realise that such a development is not a challenge to its involvement in education but rather a recognition of all people's freedom of conscience and belief as espoused by the Second Vatican Council in its own *Declaration on Religious Liberty* (1965):

> ...rooted in the social nature of man and in the very nature of religion is the right of men, prompted by their own religious sense, freely to hold meetings or establish educational, cultural, charitable and social organisations...The civil authority must therefore recognise the right of parents to choose with genuine freedom schools or other means of education. Parents should not be subjected directly or indirectly to unjust burdens because of this freedom of choice.[11]

Ethos and the Role of School Patron

The National Education Convention was held in Dublin in 1993 to promote dialogue and consensus among the various interest groups such as teachers, parents, unions and churches involved in Irish education. The work of the Convention was consolidated in the Report of the National Education Convention (1994) and again in the Government White Paper on Education, *Charting our Education Future,* (1995). The Irish Catholic Church initially welcomed both of these documents and their findings. Concerning the latter it said that:

> The White Paper acknowledged the role of the churches in education, guaranteed the continuation of denominational schools and recognised the responsibilities and the rights of the Patron/Trustees of the schools.[12]

Once again the Catholic Church here is concerned with its paternal role as manager of schools. In its response to the White Paper there is no recognition of the dynamic nature of school ethos and its implications for students' experience of school. Despite what appeared to be a consensus between State and the Church on the role of the patron, new tensions emerged after the publication of the Education Bill (1997). At their meeting in March 1997, the

Irish Bishops issued a statement claiming that, in stark contrast to the White Paper, the newly published Education Bill failed to reflect the consensus reached on the issue of patrons during the detailed consultations of the National Education Convention in 1993. The Bishops claimed that:

> The Education Bill 1997 seriously diminishes the ability of the Patrons/Trustees to fulfil their essential role. Such recognition as they are given in the Bill is either casual or constrained by regulations made by the Minister for Education.[13]

The Catholic Church sees the position of the patron as essential to its role in Irish education. Without being patron the Church would not be in such a strong position to influence the appointment of staff and other organisational decisions, which it sees as affecting the school ethos. In their responses to the Education Bill (1997), both CORI and the Irish Bishops adopted what I have already described as a custodial vision of ethos, arguing that they must be faithful to the original trust of the schools. They claimed that as patrons they are guarantors of the objectives for which the schools were established. CORI repeated this claim at the *School Culture and Ethos* conference in Dublin defining the role of patron/trustees in terms of maintaining, promoting and handing on the religious ethos, values and tradition of a particular religious community.[14] In 1997, CORI emphasises that concerns about the role of the patron in the Education Bill (1997) are not confined to denominational groups. Gaelscoileanna[15] and the multi-denominational schools would also have their role diminished under the Education Bill.[16] While CORI generally supported the Education Bill's attempts to establish regional educational boards, the Bishops accused the Government of diminishing the role of the patron in favour of increasing further State control over schools and putting funding into another layer of bureaucracy instead of schools.[17]

The debate about the role of the patron was critical to the continuing influence of the Catholic Church in Irish education. Patrons claim that in order for them to carry out their responsibilities with regard to protecting and promoting a particular ethos, it is necessary that there are procedures in place, which will enable them to work with their schools on issues related to ethos. For the moment both CORI and the Irish Bishops see no other way of maintaining the ethos of schools apart from through the role of the patron and his/her majority on the Board of Management of schools. If some other mechanism for protecting the ethos could be found both CORI and the Irish Bishops have stated that they would consider it.[18] Here, the Catholic trustees clearly see themselves in a sense as guardians of the good, with little consideration for the dynamic ongoing dimension of school ethos resulting from the ordinary dealings of the school's staff, students and teachers with each other. However, CORI does point out that it is in order to influence the school ethos rather than control it that it seeks to guarantee the role of the patron.[19] It is surprising that a pastoral institution such as the Catholic Church in Ireland has not previously explored in any great depth the idea of influencing the school ethos through the presence of professionally trained chaplains and a pastoral care professionals. Apart from a small number of religious trustees, most Catholic voluntary secondary schools still have not employed a full-time school chaplain, despite the clear success of this role in the Community/Comprehensive sector. Furthermore, research in the United States has highlighted the role of the school chaplain as the chief animator of the school's Christian ethos due to the fact that the school principal is necessarily preoccupied with matters of management.[20]

Various circumstances, including the change of government in Ireland in 1997, mean that it is hard to know exactly how successful the Church was in influencing the eventual legislation. The newly elected Government amended the Education Bill with the role of patron remaining protected while the local education boards were dropped. As in the nineteenth century, the Irish Catholic Church at the end of the twentieth century was successful in maintaining a strong position of influence in education mainly through its role as patron. However, while it has to be said that the Church articulated its educational mission honestly, the education debate of the 1990s revealed the Irish Catholic Church's vision of education to be for the most part paternalistic in terms of school management and ethos. The question has to be asked: will this paternalistic vision of education and its concern with the role of patron achieve the aims of the broader Catholic Church in terms of the Catholic school and its contribution to the life of the Church and the common good?[21] And in the light of falling vocations to the priesthood and religious life, are Ireland's lay Catholics willing and equipped to assume such a paternalistic notion of school ethos?

Ethos and School Curriculum

So far we have seen how the Catholic Church's role in Irish education, particularly in terms of the ownership and control of schools, is largely influenced by a paternalistic notion of ethos. A closer look at the internal life of Catholic schools reveals that the actual influence of the Church is somewhat weaker than it is at the level of management. This is a possible indication that in its desire to influence the ethos of schools, the Church has failed to employ an effective method other than to be involved in school management, which by its very nature tends to be removed from the ongoing life of the school. At the level of curriculum the Church now has to compete with the influence of commerce and industry as well as the media and popular fashion. Once again the Irish Catholic Church's response to curricular changes reveals a particular vision of ethos that reflects the educational language of Plato as previously outlined.

In recent years, the curriculum of the schools has been expanded by State action to include issues of morality such as family planning, Aids/HIV, drugs and sexuality which have all at least initially brought the official Irish Church into dispute with the State. According to some commentators such as Tom Inglis young Irish people today 'appear as likely to be more informed and guided in what is right and wrong by what they hear discussed in the media, as by what they are told by priests and bishops'.[22]

However, it would be far too simplistic to interpret recent changes to the curriculum as a sign of the Church losing its influence in Irish schools. As with the rest of Irish culture, the Irish

Church, particularly at grass roots level, has changed and is changing in its outlook. Many of the changes in the schools curriculum reflect the desire of most people in the Church to have an education that will help young people to interpret the experiences of the modern world in a meaningful way. Consequently, it is expected that Irish Catholics in the future will be far better equipped than they were in the past to make personal decisions in terms of morality and ethics and constant recourse to the Bishops will no longer be desirable or necessary.

However, at the level of the Irish Catholic Hierarchy, there was a considerable resistance to the State's attempt to increase its influence in the area of Relationships and Sexuality Education (RSE). Initially, the Catholic Bishops welcomed the announcement by the Minster for Education, Niamh Breathnach in 1995 that a new RSE programme would be introduced into the national curriculum for schools. However, by the time RSE came into being in 1997, it had been reduced to a set of guidelines as opposed to the full programme that had been originally expected. Although the Minister had guaranteed from the beginning that the programme would be taught within the context of each school's ethos, the Bishops wanted a further guarantee that RSE would only be taught in the Religious Education classes.[23] A compromise was eventually reached with the State agreeing that there would be no specific syllabus, but rather a set of guidelines and resource materials that would be made available to schools. Each school was to work out its own RSE policy and programme with the co-operation of parents, teachers and boards of management in the context of the schools own character or ethos.

While the Bishops had no objection to the teaching of RSE (for the most part it already formed a considerable part of the religious education programme), they were anxious that they could control the context in which it was taught. They stressed in their statement that they trusted *their* teachers to teach RSE to children in accordance with the Christian ethos of the schools. Once again, the Bishops' words and actions reflect their perception of their role as guarantors of the good with a duty to protect the young people in their care.

> In the formation of its policy [the Catholic School] should reflect the
> Catholic moral teaching on sexual matters. Even more fundamentally, it
> needs to be specific in excluding approaches which are inconsistent with the
> very foundations of Catholic moral thought.[24]

This statement implies that Catholic moral teaching on sexuality is static and it does not allow in any way for the amount of interpretation and debate that actually occurs, even within the realm of official Church teaching. It is without question that young people should seriously engage with the Catholic Church's teaching on moral issues such as relationships, sexuality and marriage. However, the Bishops approach to the RSE programme is somewhat narrow and may result in young people rejecting the values and standards put to them in schools. Effectively, the original programme intended by the Minister for Education has been subsumed into existing RSE programmes in many Irish Catholic schools. The State has minimal control over the content of RSE and the Catholic Church, as patron of most Irish schools, continues to exert its influence over the content and the manner in which RSE is taught. On the one hand, this means that RSE is taught as part of an integrated curriculum in which the young person is helped to consider the values of the Christian tradition in terms of relationships and sexuality. However, on the other hand because of the Church's paternalistic approach to RSE and to school ethos in general, one wonders to what extent students and teachers will be free to dialogue with this tradition in their classrooms.

In terms of curricular changes, the introduction of the new State-examined syllabus for Religious Education in September 2000 is probably the most significant change in education so far for the Catholic Church in Ireland. The Intermediate Education Act (1878) allowed for the teaching in Irish schools of Religious Instruction but not the examination of this subject by the State. This situation was changed as a result of a legal battle in the 1990s to allow Religious Education (RE) to be examined by the State and in early 2000 the National Council for Curriculum Assessment (NCCA) published the new Junior Certificate syllabus in Religious Education.[25] This recent development has resulted in the State, not the Church, providing the inspection and examination of a religious education programme in post-primary schools. There is an obvious opportunity for conflict here and many issues have still to be worked out such as the role of the local Bishop who up to now had been responsible through his Catechetical Advisors for the inspection of Religious Education and the suitability of teachers. While the Church does not view the religious education teachers exclusively in terms of ethos in a Catholic school, it does see them as central in achieving the goals of Catholic education.[26] The development of the examined syllabus raises questions about who can teach RE and what the role of catechetics is in the new syllabus. Overall, Irish religious educators and their representative bodies have welcomed the examined syllabus. The Bishops, while not objecting to the development of the examined syllabus, did issue strong *Guidelines for the Faith: Formation and Development of Catholic Students* (1999) in which they insisted that those who taught religion in Catholic schools should be people with a 'faith commitment' and that the nature of the teacher's professional qualification be 'theologically suitable'.[27] Once again, the Bishops' focus is paternal, seeing the teacher as someone who instructs rather than educates the student in the teachings of the Church. This contrasts with the experiential dimension of the new RE syllabus which tends to be rooted in what Devitt describes as the *Open* model of education[28] and fails to recognise the dialogue which is required if teachers are to help students to release the faith that is already within them.[29] Considering the changes in Irish society in recent times especially in relation to the practice of the Catholic faith, it seems likely that it will become more difficult in the future to find teachers who will be qualified in the way the bishops document demands. It is clear that the new syllabus allows for the teaching of religious instruction and a catechetical dimension may not always accompany this.

Having considered in this chapter the Irish Catholic Church's contribution to the great education debate of the last decade of the twentieth century, it seems to me that for the most part the official Church has taken a strongly paternalistic approach to many of the important issues now affecting our schools. When we take into account the restrictive way in which the Church had to operate before the foundations of the Irish State, it is not surprising that it developed such a paternalistic concept of ethos, seeing itself as the protector of the moral character of Irish people and their education. However, as we begin a new millennium, Ireland has become a very different place. The significant number of people who voted in favour of the legalisation of divorce in November 1995 is a clear sign that today many Irish Catholics openly differ in their views from official Church doctrine while remaining overall committed to their religion. Others have left the Church as is seen by the decreased numbers attending Mass, while others again, are members of other denominations or hold no religious faith in particular. All of this reveals a picture of Irish society that is increasingly pluralist, and consequently people's expectations and demands on schools are changing. In the face of this the leaders of the trustees of Catholic schools continue to operate out of a vision of school ethos that is over concerned with tradition and faith-fulness to the original trust of the school. To an extent, these Catholic trustees have not fully considered the role of dialogue in school ethos or the importance of the ordinary dealings of teachers, parents, and students in spontaneously developing that ethos.

Furthermore, the Catholic Church's over-reliance on the patrons' control and management as a means to influence the ethos of the schools has to a degree led to the neglect of what I call the *pastoral* option. The whole purpose of the Church's involvement is the development of the whole person as a child of God. Through the example of Jesus the teacher, as outlined previously, the Church will best influence school ethos by providing a pastoral care service in schools that seeks to develop students, emotionally, academically and spiritually. To date, pastoral care in many Irish Catholic schools is still something that is presumed to be intrinsically present but not clearly evident in the everyday life of the school. Connected to this is the development of a competitive culture and secularism in Irish Catholic schools.[30] Primary schools receive only a part-time chaplaincy service from local clergy while most Catholic voluntary secondary schools have failed to provide a full-time chaplaincy service. When Church leaders acknowledge that school ethos is something that arises spontaneously from the ordinary dealings of the members of the school community they will make it a priority to train and place personnel in schools who can be exemplars of Christianity in their care and support for teachers, parents and students helping them to dialogue with the Catholic tradition, thus contributing to the dynamic of the daily life of the school and its operational ethos.

Notes

1. Dr. Doyle, Catholic Bishop of Kildare & Leighlin, 1831, in Mulcahy, C., *Pluralism in Education, An Occasional Paper,* (Centre for Pluralism in Education, DCU, 1998).
2. Council of Thurles, 1851, 10:24.
3. O'Donoghue, T., *The Catholic Church and the Secondary School Curriculum in Ireland 1922–1962,* (New York, Peter Lang, 1999) p. 19.
4. *Ibid.* p. 20.
5. Feheney, M., *From Ideal to Action, The Inner Nature of a Catholic School Today,* (Dublin, Veritas, 1998) p. 5.
6. O'Flaherty, L., *Management and Control in Irish Education,* (Dublin, Drumcondra Teachers' Centre, 1992) p. 21, and Drudy, S., Lynch, K., *Schools and Society in Ireland,* (Dublin, Gill and Macmillan, 1993) p. 74.
7. Feheney, 1998, p. 6.
8. Bunreacht na hEireann, article 42.3.1.
9. Lynch, K., Lodge, A., *Equality in Education,* (Dublin, Gill & Macmillan, 1999) p. 248.
10. Mulcahy, C., *Pluralism in Education, An Occasional Paper,* (Centre for Pluralism in Education, DCU, 1998) p. 8.
11. Declaration on Religious Liberty, 1965, articles 4–5.
12. Irish Bishops' Conference, *Response to the Education Bill, 12/03/1997.*
13. *Ibid.*
14. McCormack, T., 'Future Directions for Trusteeship', in *School Culture and Ethos, Cracking the Code,* (Dublin, Marino 2000) pp. 153–4.
15. Primary schools dedicated to learning through the Irish language.
16. CORI, 1997, p. 19.
17. Irish Bishops, 12/03/1997.
18. National Education Convention, *Presentation of the Conference of Religious in Ireland,* (Dublin, October, 1993) p. 12.
19. *Ibid.*
20. Bryk et al, *The Catholic School and the Common Good,* (1993) pp. 146–51.
21. Grace, G., *Catholic Schools and the Common Good: What this Means in Educational Practice,* (London, IOE, 2000) p. 6.
22. Iglis, T., *Moral Monopoly, The Rise and Fall of the Catholic Church in Modern Ireland,* (Dublin, Gill and Macmillan, 1998) p. 241.
23. Irish Bishops' Conference, Statement on RSE, 23/01/95.
24. Irish Bishops' Conference, RSE Policy Document, 1997, article 3.

25. Devitt, P. *Willingly to School*, (Dublin, Veritas, 2000) p. 5.
26. *RDECS*, 1988, article 96.
27. Irish Bishops' Conference, *Guidelines for the Faith Formation and Development of Catholic Students* (Dublin, Veritas, 1999) p. 9.
28. Devitt, P., *Willingly to School*, p. 16.
29. Devitt, P., *That You May Believe*, (Dublin, Dominican Publications, 1992) p. 84–92.
30. See McDonnell, M., 'Ethos in Catholic Voluntary Secondary Schools', (UCD, unpublished Ph.D. thesis, 1995) Vol. II, p. 20.

Chapter 3

Exploring New Possibilities for School Ethos

The case can be made that, in an overlooked way, the development of the community school model over the last thirty years has already presented the Irish Catholic Church with what it claimed to be searching for at the National Education Convention in 1993: a new 'mechanism' for maintaining a Catholic ethos.

A STUDY of the relevant historical and public records, as outlined in the previous chapters, shows that the Irish Catholic Church's understanding of ethos is strongly associated with its ability to control and manage schools through a majority interest on the boards of management. In their submissions to the National Education Convention in 1993, both the Irish Bishops and the Conference of Religious in Ireland (CORI) stated that if another mechanism could be found that would allow them to protect the ethos of their schools without having a majority on a board of management, they would consider it.[1] This statement does reveal a willingness on the part of the official Catholic Church to seek another way to influence school ethos. However, to date the Church itself has failed to come up with an alternative to the paternalistic approach, which sees the issue of school ethos primarily in terms of compliance of teachers, students and all those employed in the school with officially sanctioned standards and requirements. I have already described this as a custodial or paternalistic approach to ethos, where the focus is on handing on a tradition while neglecting the educational possibilities of a dialogue with that tradition.

Research conducted by McDonnell into Catholic voluntary secondary schools has revealed that, for the most part, in acting as patron/trustee of schools, the church's role was quite weak, with over 60% of the teachers surveyed saying that the role of the trustee was removed from the ongoing (habitual) life of the school.[2] In the next chapter we will see that students in the same study identified the religious dimension of their education as the least important, after preparation for work and doing well in the Leaving Certificate. The large number of students competing for positions in third level colleges and in the workforce has led to an ethos in some Catholic schools that some researchers such as O'Keefe have described as individualistic or even secular.[3] These two findings are at odds with the educational vision of the Catholic Church, as outlined in *The Catholic School on the Threshold of the Third Millennium*, which places the development of a student's character at the heart of Christian education.[4] A more recent research project conducted by the Marino Institute of Education in 2000 on school culture and ethos in Ireland found that young people perceived academic achievement as the aspect of school life which was most valued by their school. The data from the same research also indicated that young people in Irish post-primary schools actually agreed with their schools in placing academic achievement above all other aspects of school life.[5] The findings of all of these research projects clearly presents a picture of education in Ireland, however largely Catholic, that is failing to achieve the holistic goals of education as outlined in the Vatican's post-conciliar documents.

The Community Schools

In 1966 Mr. George Colley, the Irish Minister for Education, suggested in a letter to school authorities that a time had come to look at closer co-operation between the voluntary sector and the vocational (technical) schools. In doing so the Minister was laying down the foundations of comprehensive schooling in Ireland, although it took another six years before the first Community schools as they became known were to be opened at Tallaght and Blanchardstown in County Dublin. Today, there are some 87 community schools in Ireland catering for approximately 15% of post-primary students. Although this new form of school was originally expected to be multi-denominational, O'Flaherty explains that the failure of the Irish Protestant churches to show any real interest in becoming involved with them meant that for the most part they became essentially Catholic schools.

'The final Draft Deed was considerably different from what had been proposed at the outset...Any possibility that the schools would be multi-denominational in any real sense was no longer tenable and may be attributed to the non-participation in negotiations by representatives of the Protestant denominations after 1972. What emerged was essentially a Catholic post-primary school...'[6]

As the schools were to be almost exclusively used by Catholic children, the Catholic Bishops were in a position to claim that these were actually, *de facto*, Catholic schools. For a five per cent contribution to the initial building costs the Bishops could get reserved places on the teaching staff, paid full-time Catholic Chaplains and conditions safeguarding the place of religious instruction in the school.[7] In practice, the essential difference between these community schools and the Catholic voluntary schools concerns the Church's minority interest on the boards of management of community schools. In the community schools the Catholic Church was given an opportunity to influence the ethos of the school from within the school while acting as members of the teaching staff or as Chaplains.

The case can be made that, in an overlooked way, the development of the community school model over the last quarter-century plus has already presented the Irish Catholic Church with what it claimed to be searching for at the National Education Convention in 1993: a new "mechanism" for maintaining a Catholic ethos in the schools in which it was involved. In any case, the kind of influence the Church exerts on ethos in a community school has become less paternalistic than in the voluntary secondary schools. The community school model gave religious institutions the opportunity to work in a school where for the most par t they were free from administrative concerns. The presence of these Religious and the full-time Chaplains meant that, in the case of community schools, the Irish Catholic Church was now in a position to influence school ethos through their ordinary dealings with the rest of the school community. In a community school the church's influence on school ethos is more concerned with the habitual life of the school than with the traditional managerial concept of compliance of teachers and students. Furthermore, through a presence of Religious among the Community School staff, the Church is in a position to help the school community to dialogue with the Christian tradition and if teachers, parents and students wish to, they can integrate it into their lives. The small number of Catholic voluntary secondary schools that have actually converted to community schools indicates that for the most part, the Irish Catholic Church is still reluctant to take on a form of schooling that does not give it a position of control and management. However, some have claimed that the drop in numbers of men and women joining the Priesthood and Religious Orders will eventually force the official Church into considering a greater involvement in the community school sector. Barber states:

> There is evidence that a good number of religious see their future in the community school, believing that they can best preserve and transmit their ethos through their participation in the management of such schools.[8]

However, the fact that fewer people are joining the religious life and priesthood in itself is not the only reason for the Catholic Church to consider new ways to influence the ethos of schools. In fact, the Church has always articulated the belief that the responsibilities of Catholic education belong to the whole Church and not just to members of religious communities. In the *Declaration on Christian Education*, the Church placed the primary responsibility for education within the context of the family as a right of the parents, claiming that the whole of society must support the parents in their role as principal Christian educators.[9] More recent Church documents on education, such as *The Catholic School on the Threshold of the Third Millennium*, have articulated the teaching that Christian education is best served by a partnership between all the members of the Catholic Church:

> The presence of men and women religious, side by side with priests and lay teachers, affords pupils with a vivid image of the Church and makes recognition of its riches easier.[10]

The Irish Catholic Church also affirms that the provision of Catholic schools is the responsibility of the whole Catholic community. In their recent document *The Future of Trusteeship* (1997a) the Conference of Religious of Ireland (CORI) states that despite the decline in vocations to the religious life and priesthood, the management of Catholic schools should be a shared responsibility:

> According to this kind of thinking, religious, having made a valuable contribution to establishing a network of Catholic schools, can move on to identifying and meeting urgent educational needs which cannot be met by others. Therefore many religious believe that even if the decline in membership of congregations was not taking place, it would be appropriate to begin to devise forms of trusteeship based on partnership between congregations and others.[11]

In recent years the difficulties facing some teachers, concerning the obligation to support the schools' religious character at second level or to teach Religious Instruction at primary level, have been matters for debate and negotiation.[12] In the past the Church could expect a teacher's commitment to or at least compliance with the mission of the Catholic school. However, Irish society has become more pluralist and, as Sullivan points out, the Church can no longer presume this kind of loyalty from teachers:

> The Catholic school system depends upon teachers who subscribe to the specific mission of such schools. Their contribution is expected to transcend mere verbal adherence to the leading principles of Catholic education and to embrace the role of the practical exemplar. Such an expectation meets with certain difficulties in the context of an increasingly pluralist society and within a church displaying increasingly diverse forms of self-understanding.[13]

Data from recent research carried out into the ethos of Catholic Schools in Northern Ireland has indicated that even within such a religiously polarised community, teachers in Catholic schools can have varying levels of commitment or compliance with the norms of behaviour that they perceive school management to expect.[14]

The most recent statistics reveal the number of practising Catholics, *in terms of Church attendance*, at approximately 65% compared to 91% in 1973/74.[15] If this pattern continues Irish Catholic schools may find themselves in the future in a similar situation to Catholic schools in England, where it is sometimes difficult to attract sufficient Catholic teachers to vacant posts.[16] By embracing the community school model at second level, the Irish Catholic Church would be eliminating the need to have such a high commitment from so many teachers to the religious character of the school. This does not mean that teachers in a community school are less religious than those in Catholic voluntary schools. However, a teacher who has little or no commitment to the Catholic Church will be less compromised in the community school. While the Church on the other hand is still in a position to influence the ethos of the community school through a minority interest on the Board of Management and the presence of a small number of highly committed Religious with the other teachers and a full-time school Chaplain.

Profile of Mount Seskin Community School

For the sake of this study a research project was carried out into the ethos of a particular community school in Dublin which we will call Mount Seskin Community School. The author, who was a member of the staff in Mount Seskin, carried out the research. The next chapter will present the findings of this study and compare them to the findings of similar studies into the ethos of Irish Catholic voluntary secondary schools. At this stage a profile of Mount Seskin will be presented. This profile is useful for two reasons. Firstly, it provides us with an example of the practices at work in a community school. Secondly, it is helpful at this stage to profile the school in which the research into ethos was carried out, bearing in mind the Aristotelian understanding of ethos as something that must be experienced rather than measured.

Mount Seskin Community School is set at the foot of the Dublin Mountains on the edge of Mount Seskin Parish, one of the most disadvantaged communities in the city. The co-trustees of the community school are the Daughters of Charity of St. Vincent de Paul, the Archdiocese of Dublin and the County Dublin Vocational Educational Committee (VEC). The rest of the school's board of management comprised two parents and two teacher representatives, with the school principal acting as a non-voting secretary to the board. The Daughters of Charity and the Archdiocese had been offering pastoral support to the families in the local parish since the first residents arrived when the parish was established in the late 1970s. The Daughters of Charity and the Archdiocese paid five per cent each towards the set-up costs of the school in order to become co-trustees and members of the staff selection board.

From the very beginning the Catholic Church appointed a full-time school chaplain and three Religious Sisters who took up the reserved teaching posts guaranteed in the articles of the school's Deed of Trust, the legal charter which establishes a community school. These Religious Sisters and the School Chaplain lived in the local parish thus establishing in a very real way the link between the local community and the school, as well as running youth clubs, summer camps and offering on-going support to students and their families after school hours. This kind of extra-curricular service on the part of the part of the school chaplain and the Religious was essential in the development of the new school's ethos.

In blessing and officially opening the new school building together in April 1985, the Auxiliary Bishop of Dublin, Dr. Carroll and the Minister for Education, Mrs. Hussey, signposted the relationship of partnership that was to be at the very heart of the school's ethos. The school's brochure describes the school's ethos as *'a climate of mutual respect'*. The school principal describes the ethos of the school as a place where students and teachers work together in an environment where they can both achieve their best standards. In her *Report on Discipline in Schools* Maeve Martin, who also used Mount Seskin as a research site, describes her impressions of the community school:

> Today, Mount Seskin Community School has made its mark as a highly regarded progressive Community School which provides an excellent standard of education for students of all abilities.[17]

The school motto is *'Putting Young People First'* and the school claims to achieve this by developing an excellent standard of curriculum, high realistic expectations for its students and a partnership between the home, school and community. At the time the research study into ethos was carried out, Mount Seskin had 861 students (boys and girls), 44 permanent teachers, an office staff of 3 and an ancillary staff of 11. The school also had one full-time Chaplain, a Guidance Counsellor and a Home-School-Community Liaison Co-ordinator. All teaching staff members are expected to avail of continuous in-service training in the school, so they are constantly reviewing their teaching methods so as to provide students with the most up-to-date education available.

Background Factors Affecting Ethos at Mount Seskin

There are four separate housing estates in Mount Seskin Parish, all of which are local authority (social) housing. With a population of over 7,000 people, Mount Seskin parish is larger than some Irish rural towns, yet it still lacks basic amenities such as public telephones, banks, shopping centres, cinema and swimming pools, resulting in a rather depressed atmosphere in the community. This is seen in the general untidiness of the gardens and streets. Some people live in homes with broken windows that have never been repaired. The general atmosphere of the community contributes to the low self-esteem that the students at Mount Seskin Community School often experience and this in turn can affect their academic attainment. All school boundaries, both internal and external, are highly porous. Having porous external boundaries means that it is not possible for the school to be isolated from sources of influence in the wider cultural and social environment in which the school is located.[18]

As a parish, Mount Seskin has the lowest Church practice rate of any Catholic parish in Ireland. It is estimated that less than 6% of the local population in Mount Seskin are regular Church-goers,[19] a factor that one would expect to influence the religious dimension of the school's ethos adversely. However, many of the local people continue to call on the Priests and their Parish seeking support and help, particularly in times of crisis and pain, e.g. at the sudden death of a young person, or in other periods of shock and grief.

Despite the recent growth in the Irish economy, there are still high levels of unemployment (72%)[20] and welfare dependency among the parents of the students attending Mount Seskin Community School. Subsequently, there are high levels of social problems like drug abuse, alcoholism and juvenile crime. In recent years, however, a new problem has emerged affecting student participation at Mount Seskin. Due to the strong economy, many students are being lured into unskilled jobs in the hospitality industry where they can earn significant amounts of money. Such students often have to work long hours, finishing in the early hours of the morning and consequently they either arrive in the school exhausted or do not turn up for school at all. The records in Mount Seskin Community School reveal that up to forty per cent of students could be absent on some days.

Ethos and Support for Students

Mount Seskin Community School aims to provide a support-ive and caring ethos where students are encouraged to maximise their potential. The staff at the school have developed a number of supports in an attempt to create an ethos that is pupil centred and aims to develop the whole person. These supports for students include a guidance counselling, chaplaincy, and a home-school-community liaison.

The school has two guidance counsellors who, as well as

helping students plan future careers, are also involved in supporting their access into higher education colleges. The Guidance Department operates out of a dedicated office where students can call for an appointment.

The Chaplaincy Department at Mount Seskin Community School is comprised of a full-time chaplain and a voluntary Chaplaincy Team who were trained from among the local parishioners. The support offered by the Chaplaincy Department includes, personal development retreats, liturgy and meditation, bereavement support and one-to-one counselling. Much of the Chaplaincy Department's work takes place in the school's Prayer Room or in the dedicated chaplain's Office, where there is an open door policy for students and staff. The chaplain, with the school principal, is responsible for the overall religious character of the school.

The Home-School-Community-Liaison Co-ordinator encourages parents to get involved in the school. Many courses are organised for the parents and some go on to take public examinations.

It is important to note that in terms of equality in education, School Chaplaincy is an important service that the State has still to provide in Catholic voluntary schools in the same way as it is provided in the Community School sector. Full-time paid Chaplains are currently provided in about 131 out of 751 post-primary schools. Furthermore, only schools in areas that are designated as *disadvantaged* are provided with Home-School-Community-Liaison schemes, at present there are about 350 Home-School-Community liaison schemes out of about 4,250 primary and second level schools. It is clear that if the State is to fully achieve its own objectives in terms of pastoral care, as outlined in the Education Act of 1998, it will have to significantly increase the provision of school chaplains and other pastoral supports for students and parents in Irish schools.

Ethos and Religious Education

The Catholic Church places strong emphasis on the role of the Religious Education programme in contributing to the ethos of a

Catholic School.[21] Devitt points out that the religious development of young people happens in many contexts which are distinct and yet complementary, including home, parish, school, friends and through the media. The religious character of the home is usually the most important influence on a young person's religious faith.

Where the faith of the home is weak, young people can gain insights into the riches of the Christian life through meeting good religion teachers and chaplains in school.[22] Arising from the articles of Mount Seskin's Deed of Trust, provision has been made for religious education teachers to ensure that all students receive the legal minimum number of RE classes, approximately two hours per week. Although figures from the Archdiocese of Dublin claim that about 6% of the population in Mount Seskin Parish attend church regularly, the school chaplain at Mount Seskin Community School estimates that only about 2% of students regularly attend church. A vast majority of students are baptised members of the Catholic Church. The implications of these statistics regarding church practice are significant for the teaching of RE and the overall ethos of the school. The most fundamental implication has to do with the lack of religious experiences for students outside of school hours. Teachers cannot presume that what they are teaching students is supported by any religious practices in the home. The RE teachers at Mount Seskin have described their role in terms of 'evangelisation' as they often encounter students who have received little religious formation at home.

While the teachers of RE have a very significant role to play in creating a religious ethos in a school, they are only one group within the school. Devitt highlights the contribution of pastoral care programmes, chaplaincy service, outreach groups and management's commitment to employing qualified RE teachers as important factors that contribute to the religious ethos of a school.[23] In the case of Mount Seskin Community School, there is a full-time school chaplain who offers spiritual support and pastoral care to students, staff and parents. The Chaplain also works with the RE teachers in co-ordinating religious and spiritual activities aimed at fostering the students' religious development. These activities include liturgies, meditation, and a *Faith Friends* programme with the local primary school students and other outreach activities that help students to focus on the needs of the elderly and the Developing World.

Social, Personal and Health Education

Since beginning of the school, the principal and teachers identified the need to have a comprehensive Social, Personal and Health Education (SPHE) programme, which would work alongside the RE programme. This programme has been an integral part of the school's curriculum and ethos since then. The content is directly related to student needs and covers areas of good health, personal and social skills and adolescent development. The SPHE programme is evaluated regularly and responds to the changing needs of the student population. The introduction by the Department of Education & Science of the *Relationships and Sexuality Education* (RSE) programme in 1995 has informed a review of the schools' existing policy and programme content in this area. The publication in 1998 by the NCCA of guidelines in the area of SPHE has also provided the school with an opportunity to assess and review its own health education programme.

An integral part of the SPHE programme at the school is the Tutor/Year Head system. Each class of students has its own tutor who is responsible for a number of duties pertaining to that class. In particular tutors are responsible for:

(a) Calling the register, collecting absence notes and writing up each day's attendance sheet.
(b) Encouraging proper use of the journal, signing it each week and checking that the parent has signed it.
(c) Encouraging high standards of punctuality, attendance, behaviour and neatness in the students.
(d) Promoting a sense of belonging among students in the tutor class by getting to know them as individuals.

The Year Head, who is normally an assistant principal, assists tutors in their duties as well as co-ordinating the overall running of the year group. Meetings are held between Year Heads and tutors to discuss other issues such as reports, parent/teacher meetings and the students' general well-being. The tutor may also request confidential information about a student's background in an attempt to understand him/her better. Good communication between the tutor and the Year Head, the Chaplain, Guidance Counsellor and Home-School-Community-Liaison Co-ordinator is key to the success of the pastoral care system in the school. In order to maintain good communication, all of the school's staff who are involved in pastoral care and support services meet regularly to provide an integrated approach for those students who are most at risk. Much of the school's ethos arises out of the relationship that exists between the various members of staff with responsibility for pastoral care of students.

At second level, the Community School model presents the Catholic Church in Ireland with an opportunity to influence the ethos of a school with minimum involvement in the management and administration of the school. Through the presence of the chaplain, the religious and the RE teachers among the wider teaching staff, the Church can make a significant contribution to the habitual life of the school. At the same time teachers who have little or no commitment to the Catholic Faith are more comfortable in the less paternalistic ethos of the Community School. However, for the Church, the paternalistic test of any model of education is in the school's operational ethos and the extent to which it fulfils the vision of education articulated by the Catholic Church in the various post-conciliar documents that have emerged over the last thirty-five years. In the next section I will examine to what extent the Church's involvement in a community school serves its own educational mission as outlined in these documents.

Notes

1. National Education Convention, *Presentation of the Conference of Religious in Ireland*, (Dublin, 1993) p. 12.
2. McDonnell, M., *Ethos and Catholic Voluntary Secondary Schools*, (UCD, unpublished Ph.D. thesis, 1995) Vol. II, p. 23.

3. O'Keefe, T., 'Values in a Christian School', in Feheney, M., *From Ideal to Action, The Inner Nature of a Catholic School Today*, (Dublin, Veritas, 1998) p. 40.
4. *The Catholic School on the Threshold of the Third Millennium*, (1998) article 10.
5. Furlong, C., Monahan, L., *School Culture and Ethos, Cracking the Code*, (Dublin, Marino, 2000) pp. 36–7.
6. O'Flaherty, L., *Management and Control in Irish Education: The Post-Primary Experience*, (Dublin, Drumcondra Teachers' Centre, 1992) p. 73.
7. *Ibid.*
8. Barber, N., *Comprehensive Schooling in Ireland*, (Dublin, ESRI, 1989) p. 119.
9. *Declaration on Christian Education*, (1965) articles 2–4.
10. *The Catholic School on the Threshold of the Third Millennium*, (1998) article 13.
11. CORI, *The Future of Trusteeship*, (Dublin, CORI, 1997a) p. 4.
12. INTO, *The Place of Religious Education in the National School System*, (Dublin, INTO, 1991) p. 34.
13. Sullivan, J., 'Compliance or Complaint' in *Irish Educational Studies*, Vol. 17, (Dublin, ESAI, 1998) p.183.
14. Donnelly, C., 'In Pursuit of School Ethos', in *British Journal of Education*, (London, Blackwell, June 2000) pp. 143–4.
15. The Catholic Communications Office, (Maynooth, 2001).
16. Sullivan, (1997) p. 183*ff.*
17. Martin, M., *Discipline in Irish Schools, Report to the Minister for Education*, (Dublin, Government Publications, 1997) p. 71.
18. O'Keefe, T., *Values in a Christian School*, (1998) p. 33.
19. Statistic sourced at the Communications Office of The Archdiocese of Dublin.
20. *OBAIR*, Employment Agency (Dublin, 2001).
21. *Religious Dimension of Education in a Christian School*, (1988) article 51.
22. Devitt, P., *Willingly to School*, (Dublin, Veritas, 2000) pp. 43–4.
23. *Ibid.* p. 45.

Chapter 4

Ethos and the Catholic School

It is clear from the combined research available that many Irish Catholic schools, particularly at second level, place a high value on academic achievement often to the disadvantage of the religious or pastoral development of students.

Ethos and the Catholic Voluntary School

WHILE there were some well known research projects in the US (Bryk, 1993) and in Australia (Flynn, 1979) that were concerned with aspects of ethos in the Catholic school, it is only in recent years that there has been data produced regarding this topic in Ireland. In 1995 Mark McDonnell conducted a large research project into the operative ethos of Catholic voluntary secondary schools.[1] This was followed in 1998 by Tom O'Keefe's publication of his findings from research carried out at a Catholic secondary school in the south of Ireland.[2] The year 2000 saw the publication of three reports that provided data on ethos in Catholic schools in Ireland. John Fulton published the findings of his research into the attitudes of young people in Ireland towards religion and morality, part of which included their experiences in school.[3] Caitlín Donnelly produced data from her research into the ethos of primary schools in Northern Ireland[4] and finally the end of 2000 saw the publication of data from a major survey into the ethos of Irish schools by Scott Boldt and the Marino Institute of Education.[5] As these findings are so extensive, this book does not engage in an empirical survey of a Catholic school. Instead it concentrates on a community school and uses the findings as a basis for comparison with findings from previous studies in Catholic schools.

At this stage I will develop a meta-analysis of the findings of the above research. This is useful for two reasons. Firstly, while each of these research projects was conducted using different methodologies and in different places over a number of years, as a group they provide us with an overall picture of the state of ethos in Irish schools and particularly in Irish Catholic schools. Secondly, the data from the above research will be useful for comparison and analysis with the data from the research carried out at Mount Seskin Community School.

McDonnell's research was carried out as part of a Ph.D. thesis in 1995. The researcher mostly relied on a quantitative approach relying for the most part on a very detailed questionnaire, which was completed by students and teachers in fourteen Catholic voluntary secondary schools. The schools were chosen to reflect a mix of social backgrounds, urban, rural, boys and girls. The data from McDonnell's research highlighted the inability of school management (i.e. patrons, trustees, boards of manage-ment) to influence school ethos in any major way. Most of the teachers in his survey described the trustees of the school as being removed from the ongoing life of the school. He also found that only 30% of the teachers in Catholic schools believed that the Catholic Church was offering any kind of inspirational leadership.[6]

Furthermore, overall the students and teachers in the schools surveyed by McDonnell saw the primary purpose of the school solely in terms of doing well in the Leaving Certificate and preparation for work. McDonnell reported the students in the

Catholic schools he surveyed to be 'indifferent' to Religious Education[7] and that practices in Catholic schools such as *streaming and selection* and an over emphases on academic success have resulted in an operative ethos in Catholic voluntary secondary schools that can be described as elitist, exam-focused and competitive.[8] These statistics present a major challenge to the patrons and trustees of Catholic schools in Ireland. With the numbers of religious and clergy working in schools getting lower each year, the management of Catholic schools is going to have to find a way of engaging their staff and students in a dialogue which will result in a shared vision of ethos in a Catholic school.

In his research into St. Xaviour's, a large Catholic voluntary secondary school in the southern part of Ireland, O'Keefe also relied for the most part on a questionnaire designed to compare the expectations of the parents, teachers and students in terms of the goal or purpose of the school. O'Keefe focused on expectations because he believed that the operative ethos of the school would be influenced by the values of those who make up the school community. He asked parents, teachers and students to rank in order of importance the various possible goals of the school, namely, vocational, academic, personal, religious and social.[9] The data from O'Keefe's survey was published in 1998 and he reported that when asked about their expectations of the school, parents' valued preparation for work first, with personal development second and academic development third. Parents gave their lowest ranking to the school's role in the students' religious development. While the teachers placed students' personal development first, they also gave a low ranking to religious development. The students at St. Xaviour's, like their parents, placed preparation for work as their highest priority with religious development as their lowest expectation of the school.[10] From his research at St. Xaviour's, O'Keefe concluded that the Catholic secondary school in which he carried out his research was quite individualistic and even secular.[11]

In 2000, John Fulton published data from a research project that was completed in 1999 among young Catholics in six Western countries including Ireland. The aim of the project was to compare the attitudes of these young people to religion and morality at the beginning of the new millennium. The researchers interviewed a total of fifty-five young Irish men and women all over the age of eighteen. Although the interviewees were non-randomly selected, the researchers believed that they were a fairly representative group of young adults in terms of their social background and occupations. This research among the young Catholic adults in Ireland revealed some interesting information for our topic of ethos and the Catholic school. Most of the young people interviewed described their primary school as a religious or very religious place.[12] However, Fulton reported that although most of the young people had attended secondary schools that were owned and run by Religious trustees, these schools were not often seen by the young people as religious or dominated by a religious ethos.[13] The young people in Fulton's study who had attended Catholic secondary schools described them as very academic and class conscious.[14] In the same survey, he found many of the young Catholic adults to be quite critical of their religious education at secondary school, particularly at senior cycle (last two years) where up to recently there has been no formal curriculum. The student's poor experience of religion class mirrored their growing apathy to religion as they became young adults and in fact, among the countries surveyed by Fulton for this study, Ireland had the fewest number of 'core' or committed young Catholics. On the other hand, the young people interviewed did report some positive religious experiences in school including school retreats and special Masses.[15]

The aim of Caitlín Donnelly's research was to examine the relationship between officially prescribed school ethos and that, which emerges from the social interaction within the school. While her study was not specifically confined to Catholic schools, she did differentiate her findings in the Catholic school (St. Elizabeth's) from the other school in her study. Donnelly relied on a qualitative method of research, conducting in-depth interviews and non-participant observation over a period of eight months in two primary schools. Donnelly found that there was an outward attachment to religious spirituality and authority and that this was a defining element of the school ethos even though the majority of the Religious who had taught in the school had retired.[16] While the physical environment of the school supported the *official* ethos of St. Elizabeth's, she also found that the personal beliefs of staff and governors frequently departed from the official aims of the school. School governors, parents and teachers spoke of the personal conflict generated by the 'disparity between their own values and attitudes as compared to those upheld in the school'.[17] At the time of Donnelly's investigation, staff and governors at the school were 'unwilling to challenge openly the prevailing ethos of the school underlining the importance of outward conformity, to a set of religious and traditional ideals'.[18] This reflects McDonnell's earlier research, which found that teachers were generally unwilling to challenge the status quo in Catholic schools.

Scott Boldt's study into the ethos of Irish schools was not specifically concerned with Catholic schools. However, it is by far the largest study on school ethos in Ireland and its findings, taken with the fact that the majority of Irish schools are Catholic in one form or another (see chapter 2), help to complete the picture of ethos in Irish Catholic schools. Parents, teachers and students in this study completed a total of 1,279 questionnaires. These questionnaires were designed to explore the concept and experience of school culture and ethos. This study found that students in both primary and post-primary schools perceived their schools to value 'an ethic of hard work' and 'academic achievement' more than anything else. The study also suggests that students themselves held the same values as their schools regarding hard work and academic achievement.[19] Students, parents and teachers all gave a low ranking to Christian values in terms of the schools actual and ideal ethos. So, even though this study was not principally concerned with Catholic schools, its findings are important in that as with the other studies, it suggests that most Irish schools value academic achievement most and religious or Christian development least.

Boldt does point out that just because an item, such as religious development, is given a low ranking does not necessarily indicate that it is not valued but that possibly teachers, students and parents value other things more.[20] The data from this study also indicated that while the majority of teachers think that they should ideally spend more time helping students with personal and pastoral problems they actually spend most of their time 'encouraging academic achievement and addressing pupil discipline'.[21] The majority of respondents in this study described ethos in terms of core values that determine the life of the school or what the trustees of the school determine to be the aims, values and conduct of the school. Boldt concluded that many parents and students do not see themselves as contributors to the ethos of their school.[22]

It is clear from the combined research available that many Irish Catholic schools, particularly at second level, place a high value on academic achievement often to the disadvantage of the religious or pastoral development of students. It is not surprising that Catholic schools in Ireland have developed this academic culture when we consider the historic perception in Ireland of education as the key to personal and national development. What is surprising is that the trustees of Catholic schools have largely failed to maintain, along side the academic focus, a religious ethos in their schools, allowing them to develop an ethos that can be described as secular.

Ethos and the Community School

As described in the previous chapter, Community schools in Ireland, though comprehensive in nature, have evolved as *de facto* Catholic schools due to the high proportion of Catholics who use these schools not to mention the minority involvement of the Church on boards of management as well as the presence of Religious and Chaplains on the staff. I will now outline the research undertaken between 1998-9 at Mount Seskin Community School. The purpose of this research was to find out, in terms of ethos, if the aims of the Catholic Church in education as outlined in the documents to follow the Second Vatican Council can be achieved in a Community School where the Church has adopted a less paternalistic role in management and a more pastoral role within the life of the school itself.

As with many of the studies outlined above, a sociological model of the school was devised. This model identified the parents, students and teachers as the primary agents of ethos in the school. In order to evaluate the operational ethos of the school, it was decided firstly, to examine the expectations of the parents, teachers and students in terms of the goals of the school and secondly to examine their experience of the school in terms of the tutor system and religious education programme.

As mentioned previously, the goals of a school can be classified into three types: instrumental, organisational and expressive. While a school may try to hold a balance between the different types of goals it will have, one type of goal may dominate, often as a result of pressures inside and outside of the school. For example, in recent years Irish schools have come under a lot of pressure from the industry and the economy to provide young people with the skills to enable them to enter the workforce quickly. This has often resulted in many schools spending more time on science and mathematical subjects *(instrumental order)* than on other activities such as school plays and debating which will help to develop the student's character *(expressive order)*. Dunne has argued among others that over the last twenty years or so Irish education has experienced a displacement of its expressive goals for the sake of the more instrumental ones. As he explains, the dynamic by which goals are evaluated and prioritised occurs both within and without the school in particular from society, industry, and the State.[23] In this study we see how parents, students and teachers can evaluate educational goals in different ways, each having their own expectations of the purpose of the school. In the working out of these expectations a dominant value system arises, which in turn determines the spirit or ethos of the Catholic school.

The research participants were drawn from the parents, teachers and students at Mount Seskin Community School. Parent research was by way of small focus groups to which a random representative group of parents where invited. The researcher conducted these meetings at which the parents were asked to complete a questionnaire concerning their expectations of the school and given a chance to discuss their experience of the school in terms of the tutor system. At the same time all of the school's teaching staff (44) were asked to complete two questionnaires, the first concerning their expectations of the school and the second concerning the class tutor system at work in the school. Twenty teachers agreed to take part in short interviews regarding their answers on the first questionnaire.

The first questionnaire was also administered to final year students, asking them about their expectations of the school. Furthermore, over a number of weeks around the time the students were asked to complete the questionnaires, the researcher conducted small focus group sessions with 100 (75%) Leaving Certificate students in which the students were asked to elaborate on their opinions regarding the goals of the school and their experience of the tutor system and the religious education programme. A random selection of students of all abilities, about 30% of each year group, was also asked to complete a question-naire that was designed to evaluate their experience of the class tutor system in the school.

Vocational Development

The results of the study at Mount Seskin Community School present a picture of ethos that is considerably different from that of the Catholic voluntary schools presented above. Only 18% of the students at Mount Seskin specified preparation for employment as the most important purpose of the school. This 18% figure is considerably lower than the 36.9% of students in the McDonnell (1995) study into Catholic voluntary secondary schools, who regarded preparation for work as the most important purpose of the school. In the study by O'Keefe (1998), preparation for work was also stated as the most important expectation of students. The fact that only 18% of students at Mount Seskin Community School ranked preparation for work first, can probably be explained by the fact that many of the students at Mount Seskin Community school already hold down part-time jobs and have therefore, not made the link between education and future employment.

If the students at Mount Seskin considered the school's role in preparation for work of little importance, the teachers at Mount Seskin gave it even less of a priority with only 8% choosing it as the first purpose of the school. This statistic may be explained in the light of the school's emphases on SPHE and the consequent style of education in the school. In interviews with the researcher, teachers explained how they saw the purposes of the school in terms of a hierarchy of needs.[24]

Similarly only 14% of parents at Mount Seskin said that they saw the school in primarily in terms of their son or daughters future employment. This contrasts with the study by O'Keefe who found that the highest priority for the parents in the school he studied was preparation for work. Once again, we must take into account the background factors affecting the values of the parents, teachers and students at Mount Seskin. The high level of unemployment in the local area must be taken into account when considering these statistics. The fact that the students, teachers and parents at Mount Seskin display a relatively low expectation of the school's role in preparation for work indicates the kind of impact that the character of the local area can have on the ethos of a school.

Academic Development

The student's success in the workforce will to a large extent depend on their success in the Leaving Certificate and their ability to gain access to third-level education. It is not surprising then that a total of 31% of the students at Mount Seskin Community School chose success in the Leaving Certificate as the most important thing the school could do for them. In terms of school ethos, McDonnell concluded that the Catholic secondary schools in his study were quite secular due to the fact that 58% of the students he surveyed saw the purpose of the school in terms of preparation for work and getting a good Leaving Certificate.[25] The statistic from Mount Seskin indicates that the ethos there is considerably less academic than the ethos in the Catholic secondary schools studied by McDonnell.

Turning to the teachers' responses, only 4% believed that the most important thing the school could do for its students was to help them to do well in the Leaving Certificate or get a place in college. This figure is significantly lower than the high number of teachers in the other studies outlined at the start of this chapter who saw academic success as a priority for their schools. Over the years the teachers at Mount Seskin have continually evaluated their role in terms of student needs. Teachers stated in their interviews that, in addressing the students' personal development first, as well as health and social skills, they hope that the education they offer will be more relevant to the students and the wider context of their lives. It is no surprise then, that students were observed by the researcher to relate to teachers in a personal and respectful manner and this in turn can be seen to effect the overall character of the school.

The parents at Mount Seskin Community School gave a much higher priority (22%) to the school's role in helping the students to achieve in the Leaving Certificate than was given by the teachers of the school. It seems then, that overall the concern with academic achievement at Mount Seskin is quite low compared to the other studies outlined previously. Arising from this we must ask does the apparent low priority given by parents, teachers and students at Mount Seskin to academics result in the school ethos being depressed or is it that the school's priorities are focused on something other than academics?

Personal Development

While only 17% of the students at Mount Seskin stated that the first purpose of the school was to help students understand themselves, develop their personality and a sense of independence, the teachers at the school gave it their highest priority with 52% of them seeing personal development as the most important thing they could do for their students. In terms of personal development, the teachers at the school have gone to great lengths to achieve their goals by developing a class tutor system that is aimed at helping the students to develop themselves while in school.

The parents at Mount Seskin Community School were equally concerned with their children's personal development, with 52% of them stating that personal development was their highest expectation of the school. When we consider the Church's contribution to the ethos at Mount Seskin, it is interesting to note the involvement of the Religious Sisters in the school in terms of students' personal development. One of the Sisters runs a school choir, which serves as a vehicle for personal development of over seventy students. In the choir the students not only learn music and singing but they also are helped to develop their self-esteem and confidence and qualities of respect for self and others, as well as expressing their personality. Another Sister co-ordinates an after-school youth club for students in which they partake in activities aimed at developing their self-esteem. Furthermore, the school chaplain co-ordinates in-school pro-grammes aimed at the personal development of the students such as the bereavement support group and school retreats. He is also available for counselling.

Social Development

Only 8% of the students at Mount Seskin Community School specifically stated that they believed the most important thing the school could do for them was to help them develop their social skills, a sense of community spirit and a concern for the needs of others. This compares equally with the students in the other Irish studies who also gave a low ranking to social development.[26] However, when we take together, the 25% of students at Mount Seskin Community School, who prioritised social and personal development, they are significantly higher than the 18% who made the same choice in the Catholic secondary schools studied by McDonnell.[27] While it is true that more students at Mount Seskin ranked doing well in the Leaving Certificate and getting a job as their most significant expectations of the school, there still seems to be a higher number of them, compared to the students in the Catholic secondary schools, with an expectation of the school's role in their personal and social development.

Over 32% of the teachers at Mount Seskin stated that the most important thing the school could do for its students was to help them develop their social skills and a sense of community spirit. However, if we add this figure to the teachers who prioritised personal development, we find that 84% of the teachers identified personal and social development as the most important thing the school could do for the students. When this is compared with the 16.7% of teachers in the McDonnell study who prioritised the social and personal aspect of education,[28] it seems that there is a much higher awareness of the students' social and personal needs among the teachers at Mount Seskin than there is in the schools studied by McDonnell. In placing social development fourth in order of priority (10%), the parents at Mount Seskin compared equally to their counterparts in the Catholic secondary school studied by O'Keefe where parents and teachers also placed social development fourth after preparation for work, doing well in the Leaving Certificate and personal development (McDonnell did not include parents in his study). When we add the number of parents at Mount Seskin who identified the importance of personal and social development together, we find that 62% of the parents at Mount Seskin are anxious that their children develop their identity and self-esteem while understanding the society in which they live.

Overall, the parents and teachers at Mount Seskin can be said to have given considerable importance to the social and personal dimensions of education. These findings reflect the effort that has gone into the various pastoral initiatives at Mount Seskin that are aimed at students' personal and social development. The year head and tutor system, the chaplaincy team and the SPHE programme have all been put in place in order to help student's develop their self-esteem and meaningful relationships. Consequently, we can say that a large part of the operative value system that is at the centre of Mount Seskin's spirit or character is student-centred and that the school is as its brochure claims *"putting young people first"*. Furthermore, the ethos at Mount Seskin Community School can be said to reflect the objectives of the Catholic Church in education as stated in the *Catholic School on the Threshold of the Third Millennium*, in that through the tutor system and the other support services at the school, students are educated through the personal relations that they experience with their teachers.[29]

Religious and Spiritual Development

Just 11% of the students at Mount Seskin ranked religious ad spiritual development as their first expectation of the school. This figure is considerably higher than the 0.9% of students in McDonnell's study who saw the religious dimension of their school as important. This is interesting considering the very low ranking given to religious and spiritual development by the teachers (4%) in Mount Seskin compared with the 28.3% of teachers in the McDonnell study who specifically described their school's purpose in terms of religious development. In their interviews with the researcher, the teachers at Mount Seskin gave two reasons for giving such a low ranking to religious development. Firstly, teachers felt that they were not competent to contribute to students' religious or spiritual development in any direct way. Many of them regarded this as a specialist area that was taken care of by the RE teachers and the school chaplain. Secondly, a larger group articulated their belief that the school must first help students to develop the more basic needs such as social and personal skills before it could develop students at a 'higher' level such as the religious or spiritual level.

In other words, the fact that teachers gave a low ranking to the role of the school in the religious development of students does not mean that religious development is not a important role for the school to take on. Rather, it means that the teachers considered that the students had more fundamental needs that should be addressed first. As with the parents in the study by O'Keefe, the parents at Mount Seskin also gave their lowest ranking to religious development. This probably reflects the wider change in Irish society where religious practice is concerned.

In the focus group meetings with students, most of them declared that they enjoyed the RE classes at the school. The Leaving Certificate students at Mount Seskin stated clearly that their RE classes should not be cancelled or replaced with some other subject. All but one of these final year students talked about God, using words like, 'loving', 'caring', and 'father', to describe him. When asked specifically about the different elements of the RE programme being used in the school, students distinguished between religious instruction (RE class) and the spiritual education programmes such retreats and meditation in the school prayer room. Most of them spoke positively about meditation and prayer experiences with the chaplain in the school prayer room and all of them described their retreats in the following terms.

- 58% said that their school retreat helped them to reflect on their life.
- 68% said the retreat helped them to focus on their future.
- 68% said that the retreat helped them think about their relationships with other people.
- 55.1% said that their relationships with other people had improved since the retreat.
- 31% said that the retreat helped them to think more about their relationship with God.
- 69% said that the retreat was overall a positive experience for them.

The above information reflects the comments of the young Catholic adults in the study by Fulton,[30] when they highlighted school retreats as a positive element of their school's RE programme. Furthermore, we can say that in this study when asked to describe the purposes of the school, Leaving Certificate students did give a lower ranking to religious and spiritual development than to other aspects of their education. However, the focus groups reveal that religious and spiritual education forms an important part of the educational experience at Mount Seskin and that these students give it more significance than their counterparts in the Catholic voluntary secondary schools that were described as being indifferent to religious education by McDonnell.[31]

Evaluation of Class Tutor System

The above analysis of the data from the study carried out at Mount Seskin reveals an overall expectation on the part of the parents and teachers and to a lesser extent the students that the school will contribute in a significant way to the pastoral development of the students. While these expectations can be said to contribute greatly to the ethos of the school, the extent to which members of the school feel their expectations are realised gives a greater indication of the spirit at Mount Seskin Community School. The data from the second questionnaire on the class tutor system gives an indication of the extent to which people's pastoral expectations are met at Mount Seskin.

In relation to the class tutor system it was found that 78-80% of class tutors could give a short biographical note on students in relation to their personal strengths and weaknesses. A further 57% of tutors at Mount Seskin were aware of each of their student's home situations while 70% of the tutors said that they continually monitor the social relationships of the students in their class-groups. On the students' side, 93% of first year and 66% of final year students who took part in the study said that their tutor had helped them with a personal difficulty in school such as conflicts with other students, relations with teachers and bullying. A further 55% of first year and 56% of final year students said that their tutor had helped them with personal problems at home. In addition, 83% of the first years and 88% of final years said that their tutor had helped them to fit into the school. These results reveal a positive relationship between students and teachers. Considering that all of the survey on the tutor system was designed with the school's policy document on the role of the tutor in mind, the above statistics reveal a very high satisfaction rate among students with the class tutor system in Mount Seskin.

Overall, the data from Mount Seskin Community School indicates that the school's value system places students' personal and social development as its highest priority. Whereas the other studies into Catholic schools all presented a picture of an ethos in Catholic schools that was overly concerned with academic development. It is reasonably clear from the results of the study at Mount Seskin that not only do the parents, students and teachers expect the school to contribute to the students' personal and social development, but that they actually believe that the school's pastoral care system is meeting this expectation. Consequently we can conclude that Mount Seskin Community School is achieving its overall goal of putting young people's development at the centre of the life of the school. The operational ethos of the school is one where students are encouraged to do their best without undue academic pressure. Furthermore, while Mount Seskin could not be described as an overly religious place, the final year students did display a considerably more positive attitude towards religion than their counterparts in the studies by McDonnell and by O'Keefe who where described as 'indifferent to religion' and 'secular'. It is clear that the community school model is at least as good if not better than the voluntary secondary school in creating an ethos that meets the holistic aims of education and that part of this success is due to the type of *hands-on* presence that the official Church holds in a community school.

Notes

1. McDonnell M., *Ethos in Catholic Voluntary Secondary Schools*, (Dublin, UCD, unpublished Ph.D. Thesis, 1995).
2. O'Keefe, T., 'Values in a Christian School', in Feheney, *From Ideal to Action, Inner Nature of a Catholic School*, (Dublin, Veritas, 1998).
3. Fulton, J., et al., *Young Catholics at the New Millennium*, (Dublin, UCD Press, 2000).
4. Donnelly, C., 'In Pursuit of Ethos', in *British Journal of Education*, (London, June, 2000) pp. 134–54.
5. Boldt, S., 'A Vantage Point of Values – Findings from School Culture and Ethos Survey Questionnaires', in Furlong C., Monahan, L., *School Culture and Ethos, Cracking the Code*, (Dublin, Marino, 2000) pp. 29–58.
6. McDonnell, (1995) Vol. II, p. 451.
7. *Ibid.* p. 446.
8. *Ibid.* p. 434.
9. O'Keefe, p. 31*ff*.
10. *Ibid.* p. 34.
11. *Ibid.* p. 40.
12. Fulton, p. 56.
13. *Ibid.* p. 57.
14. *Ibid.*
15. *Ibid.* p. 59.

16. Donnelly, p. 141.
17. *Ibid.* p. 143.
18. *Ibid.* p. 145.
19. Boldt, pp. 36–7.
20. *Ibid.* p. 36.
21. *Ibid.* p. 41.
22. *Ibid.* pp. 41–2.
23. Dunne, J., 'What's the Good of Education', in Hogan, P., in *Partnership and the Benefits of Learning, Symposium,* (Dublin, ESAI, 1995) p. 66.
24. Maslow, A. *Towards a Psychology of Being,* (1968).
25. McDonnell, (1995) Vol. II, p. 19.
26. *Ibid.* p. 17*ff* and O'Keefe, p. 37.
27. *Ibid.* p. 19.
28. *Ibid.* p. 17.
29. (1998) Article 18.
30. Fulton, p. 59.
31. McDonnell,'Ethos' Vol. II, p. 446.

Chapter 5

Pastoral Care and Teachers

Through the development of a personal integration of values, empathy with pupils and colleagues, vision and adaptability teachers are seen to posses a professional attitude and so enhance the ethos of the school.

Introduction

WE have reached a stage, in terms of our thinking, where life is characterised by the process of questioning rather than the attainment of answers. This time has been described as *post-modernity*, a time in which rigid boundaries are shifting and many previously held ideas are in a constant state of flux, seeking to respond to the changing world in which they are applied. In this context our notion of schooling has developed considerably and this in turn has impacted on the expectations we place as a community on those who teach.

In recent years the curriculum has seen many additions, which have raised our expectations of the goals of education and the role of the teacher. This is reflected in the pastoral goals of recent legislation, which obliges schools to promote the *'moral, spiritual and personal'* development of the pupil.[1] New syllabi such as *Social*

Personal and Health Education (SPHE), *Civic Social and Personal Education* (CSPE) and *Relationships and Sexuality Education* (RSE) have been introduced to promote pupils' social and personal needs and to provide a balance to the pervading academic ethos of Irish schools.[2] Despite the fact that these initiatives have been introduced during a relatively short period of time onto an already overloaded curriculum, teachers have for the most part responded wholeheartedly to them.

However, debates such as those during the industrial dispute in Ireland between the teachers' union and the government[3] highlight the fact that our notions of teacher professionalism are quite fluid and it can be hard at times to arrive at a common understanding of what it means to be professional and to be a teacher.

In this chapter I wish to reflect on the impact of the developments mentioned above for the professional nature of teaching in Ireland. On the one hand, the introduction of so many new school programmes means that there is a danger that teachers will become a jack-of-all-trades and master of none and so undermine their professional integrity. On the other hand, these new programmes may be seen as extending the teacher's role and enhancing teacher professionalism. This chapter will address two questions, firstly in what sense can teachers be described as professionals and secondly is pastoral care a necessary dimension of teacher professionalism in Ireland?

In exploring these issues I am aware that the concept of pastoral care is not as strongly associated with teaching in other countries as it is in Ireland and Britain. For example, since World War II in Germany, somewhat in reaction to the Nazis, the remit of the school decreased in favour of the family's responsibility for personal and social education. Even today, Giesecke warns that any attempt in Germany to compensate for the failings of society would put such a strain on the education system that it would fail.[4] On the other hand, in both Britain and Ireland personal and social development has long been established as an important dimension to schooling and teachers' work.[5] Consequently, this chapter will not argue for or against but take as a given that schools in Britain and Ireland have a strong duty of care and instead will explore the relationship between teacher professionalism and pastoral care of pupils.

There has been a considerable amount of writing on the topic of professionalism.[6] However, for the purpose of this paper I will mainly draw on some insights on the concept of professionalism as applied to teaching by Hargreaves and Goodson (1996) Gaden (1988) and Williams (2001). Regarding the literature on pastoral care and education, I will develop my insights based on works by Best (1999) Collins (1999) and Campbell (2000).

Are Teachers Professionals?

Mainstream professions such as medicine, law and the clergy have been characterised by their claim to have a specialised knowledge or shared technical culture, an ethic of public service and a high degree of autonomy in a practice that is regulated by a self-governed collegial body.[7] Despite some well-reported cases of bad practice in some of the above professions[8] which were in some way allowed to happen due to their lack of accountability to those outside the profession, there is still a tendency among other occupations such as teaching to use the conventional characteristics of a profession like medicine as a benchmark for judging their own professional worth.

Although in Ireland the public has traditionally conferred a professional status on the teacher along with the local priest and doctor, a further examination of teaching in the light of the professional qualities mentioned above will reveal that teachers do not necessarily rely on a specialist knowledge to the same extent as those engaged in medicine and or who are members of the clergy. Kevin Williams compares the role of the teacher with that of a doctor and the degree to which each requires specialist knowledge to achieve their occupational aims. He argues that in teaching a pupil about the atom for example, *'teachers do not need to know about higher order scientific exploration of why their procedures have the effects they have'.*[9] Good teachers will simply employ a number of strategies until they find one that helps the pupil to learn.

I can illustrate this point by recalling an experience I had in a school where I was a member of the Board of Management. The principal reported that the science results for that year's Junior Certificate examinations were higher than previous years despite the fact that the newly appointed temporary teacher had no formal educational qualification. She did of course hold a science degree and was an innovative communicator, for example, using empty soft drink cans to teach concepts such as the cylinder to her pupils. Although I am not advocating that unqualified teachers become the norm in our schools, I am suggesting that, apart from their own teaching subject, teachers do rely less on specialist knowledge than doctors who would be arrested if they were to experiment on their patients to find out which treatment will work. Williams points out that *'however complex the skill of teaching may be, the explanatory theory available to teachers is much less than that available to doctors'*.[10]

Consequently, I would suggest that the apparent professional status conferred in the past by the public on teachers in Ireland probably had more to do with the perception by a largely uneducated public that teachers were the gatekeepers to knowledge and ultimately freedom from poverty than it had to do with their technical competence. If teachers cannot claim ownership of specialist knowledge, as doctors can, then in what sense can they claim to be professionals?

Professionalism and Professional Attitudes

As already noted, the traditional conceptions of what it means to be professional can be problematic, especially as their closely guarded autonomy and self-regulation have often allowed roguish practitioners such as serial killer Dr. Harold Shipman and paedophile Fr. Brendan Smith to transgress the ethical limits of their professions without question. Furthermore, in these post-modern times, when previously held certainties are being questioned and boundaries are constantly changing, it seems that there is a need to reconceptualise our ideas of what it means to be a professional. It is in this context that the term *professionalism* has come to be identified with both the maintenance of an ethos of high standards in schools and, more fundamentally, with an attitude that marks the relationship between the practitioner and the client such as the teacher and the pupil.[11] While we have formal structures such as the Leaving Certificate examination to measure standards in teaching in terms of cognitive development, it is not so clear how we can measure the extent to which a teacher has a professional attitude, which, arguably, is at the heart of a positive teacher pupil relationship and will promote a positive ethos in the school. Gerry Gaden describes a professional attitude as:

'...a complex of dispositions and tendencies, with underlying beliefs and commitments, which broadly determines the manner and spirit in which the practitioner carries on in his occupation.'[12]

While the concept of a 'professional attitude itself may be somewhat elusive, it is possible to identify some fundamental conditions that teachers will need to possess if they are to develop the professional attitude that is required to develop a good personal relationship with their pupils and to contribute to a successful school ethos.

I will now expand on the above definition of a professional attitude by exploring some of the underlying conditions that promote a professional attitude among teachers.

Integrity

Firstly, it is argued that the teacher with a professional attitude will possess a high degree of *integration* between the values that influence their personal and professional self. Gaden calls this condition 'authenticity', remarking that *'self and work do not have to be the wholly identified, but they cannot be wholly cut off'*.[13] In other words teachers can be said to have a professional attitude when they maintain a level of continuity between their private and public life. Similarly, in identifying personal relationships as central to effective teaching, Karl Rogers wrote about the need for the teacher to be a *'real person...without presenting a front or facade'*.[14] In the past the integration between a teacher's personal and professional life was promoted by the fact that teachers lived in the communities where they worked. They were identified by others and by themselves as 'the master' or 'the mistress' and viewed as upright people who could be relied on to provide leadership and stability in the community as well as educating children in school. Furthermore, because the school was so closely linked to the local community, its boundaries were porous in that events in the local community often spilled over into the life of the school. The annual harvest or in Irish *'meitheal'* is an example of the integration of school and community, whereby the school would suspend lessons so that the pupils could help in the work on the farms.

Today teachers are more likely to travel many miles to their schools and consequently, the integration that is required for them to have a professional attitude towards their work will be harder to achieve in that, like others, teachers' lives are becoming more fragmented and consequently the connection between self and work is not as apparent as in the past. If a gap develops between a teacher's personal and professional identity, s/he is in danger of seeing their work merely in terms of salary or *just a job* and thus be less likely to successfully develop positive relationships with their pupils and even undermine the ethos of the school. Authenticity here means that I believe in what I am doing as a teacher and that it is important to me. If teachers are to be successful in their work and develop a professional attitude they need to achieve a consistency between the value judgements made in professional practice and in the rest of their lives. This may appear to be overly demanding on teachers when compared to other occupations, but imagine the situation if it was not the case. At the heart of teaching is a relationship that is based on trust and respect. If teachers promoted a value system in schools that they do not believe in or actually apply in their own lives this could result in them being accused of hypocrisy or double standards and so undermine the teacher–pupil relationship.

Empathy

Secondly, teachers who establish strong relationships with their pupils have an ability to take into account their pupil's experiences and perspectives and this awareness of their pupils personal experiences and perspectives can influence the teachers approach to how their pupils will learn. Consequently, it can be argued that *empathy* is an essential condition for the development of a professional attitude among teachers. Cooper defines empathy as:

> 'A quality shown by individuals, which enables them to accept others for who they are, to feel and perceive situations from their perspective and to take a constructive and long-term attitude towards the advancement of their situation, by searching for solutions to meet their needs.'[15]

Empathy has been identified as a key factor in the development of a child's moral growth.[16] However, the acquirement of empathy depends on the extent to which the child has been shown empathy by other significant adults including teachers. Thus, empathy is not just important for the development of a professional attitude between the teacher and the pupil but it is also essential if the pupil is to develop as a moral being. Teachers who spend time getting to know and understand their pupils develop an attunement with them that is realised in close relationships, good behaviour and positive modelling.[17]

Vision

Thirdly, a professional attitude is *informed* by developments in educational theory and developing educational policy on curriculum and best practice in teaching as well as an awareness of what is recognised as the common good of education. In other words, it is not professional for a teacher to do just anything in their work that is not rationally defensible. For Gaden this 'defensibility' has to do with'certain *"realism with regard to the main structural features of the occupation and its context"*.[18] A teacher who can justify their practice in terms of the agreed aims of education can be said to have a developed a certain professionalism in their work. The recently developed *School Planning and Development Initiative* in Irish schools may provide a forum in which teachers and school managers can reflect on and articulate the rationale behind their practice and so further develop the concept of professionalism in education.

Adaptability

The final condition required for the development of a professional attitude is *adaptability*. While the practitioner may be guided by an awareness of current theory and best practice in education, they are also responsive to the changing circumstances of the work place.[19] Pupils become ill, they get upset or they can have bad days when, sometimes as a result of stress at home, they are unable to concentrate and learn. Their distress may even express itself in disruptive behaviour in the classroom. Teachers who take a purely *'reactive'* stance by punishing this type of behaviour are shortsighted in that they are ignoring the causes.[20] Furthermore, discipline programmes that are narrowly linked to the behaviourist school of psychology such as *Discipline For Learning*[21] could be said to undermine the adaptable nature of a teacher's professionalism in that they demand a conformity of approach to all students in every situation. These programmes also undermine the holistic aims of education as set out in recent legislation (Education Act 1998, 9d), in that they fail to respect the individuality of each student and the impact of their home life on their ability to succeed in school. Adaptability is an important skill for a teacher in the development of a professional attitude towards their pupils in that it allows them to respond to their pupils emerging needs as they arise in the context of the classroom.

In so far as teachers possess the four core conditions outlined above, they can be said to be professionals. However, their professionalism cannot be learned from a book in the same way as a doctor might learn medicine. These four conditions, *integration, empathy, vision* and *adaptability* are not a prescriptive list that can be followed in order to achieve a professional attitude; they come from within a person's character. The challenge for those involved in teacher training and ongoing development is how to develop this type of character in teachers? For Aristotle goodness of character (*éthos*) was achieved through habit (*êthos*). In other words, a teacher acquires a professional attitude through habitual interaction with other good teachers.[22] This interaction may begin while the teacher is still a pupil in school and continues through his/her training and induction and afterwards during his/her teaching career. In this way, we can say that teachers have a professional worth that goes much deeper than any claim to a specialist knowledge or status that the public may or may not confer on them. Teacher professionalism comes from character and is fundamental to the development of personal relationships with pupils. Furthermore, these personal relationships are a key factor in the promotion of pastoral ethos in schools.

Nature of Pastoral Care and Teaching

Having shown how teachers may be considered as professionals in a way that is fundamentally different from those who work in medicine or law, I will now explore to what extent pastoral care is a professional characteristic of teaching. From my own experience working in second-level schools, this is an important question to be explored because while most teachers have overwhelmingly embraced the pastoral aims of recent legislation, there are others who argue that they should not be expected to become 'counsellors' and that they should be left to get on with the business of teaching. These teachers have been described as 'anti-collectivists' who at most view pastoral care as a means of controlling pupils whose behaviour is unacceptable to them.[23] While these anti-collectivists represent a small number of teachers, they do challenge the rest of us to be able to articulate a defence of the relationship between pastoral care and teacher professionalism. For the rest of this chapter I will try to present such a defence by exploring the link between pastoral care and teaching.

There is hardly a school in Ireland that doesn't claim to offer pastoral care to its pupils. Apart from the specialist care offered by school chaplains and guidance counsellors, recent research indicates the majority of pupils' pastoral needs are met by the classroom teacher.[24] However, teachers have many perceptions of what it means to be involved in pastoral care. For some teachers it means the provision of a Social, Personal and Health Education programme. For others, pastoral care refers to the role of the head of year, the class tutor, and the chaplain or guidance counsellor. It is sometimes understood as being part of the Religious Education programme or a way of describing the 'good' teacher. Úna Collins has defined pastoral care as:

> 'that which the student experiences in their school life. It is the spirit, the culture, the heart of the school. It is the recognition, respect and support which each student can claim as a right and as a responsibility within the learning community.'[25]

The vagueness of this particular definition reflects the elusiveness of pastoral care as a concept in Irish second-level schools. However, for the purposes of this chapter, I will attempt to provide an etymology of the term and describe it as I have experienced it in second-level schools in Ireland.

The word 'pastoral' (*pascere*), meaning Shepard, is biblical in origin and was used as a metaphor for the relationship between God and his people (Isaiah 40:11, Ezekiel 34:16). In the New Testament, the term 'pastoral' (*poimen*) is applied to Jesus Christ to describe his care and concern for God's people, particularly those who are lost or outcast (Luke 15: 1-8). In the Bible and the early Christian Church, the term 'pastoral' was used to describe the care of God or his representative for his people. In this context, the term 'pastoral care' describes a faith action, that is an action carried out by a person of faith for another person.[26]

In the 1960s and 1970s when comprehensive schooling was developing in Ireland teachers looked to Britain, as our nearest neighbour, where this type of schooling had already been established since the 1950s.[27] Consequently, the model of pastoral care in British comprehensive schools greatly influenced the development of pastoral care as a formal concept for teachers in what was to become the Community/Comprehensive schools and later on in the voluntary secondary schools. However, it has been argued that in an informal way pastoral care as we now know it has always been part of the good school and the work of the good teacher in Ireland.[28] It is also important to note that the fact that there was no legislative obligation on schools in Britain to promote pupil's spiritual development until quite recently[29] meant that their pastoral care structures tended to neglect this aspect of education.[30] To a certain extent this has influenced a common perception among some teachers in Ireland that pastoral care is not concerned with anything religious or spiritual. Furthermore, the lack of any mention of the term 'pastoral care' in official literature in Ireland until quite recently[31] meant that, at times, teachers engaged in pastoral care without any formal training and without a language to express what they were doing. This often resulted in the perception that pastoral care was the 'soft option' and had less to do with teacher professionalism than academic work and maintaining discipline in the classroom. The establishment of postgraduate courses for teachers in pastoral care, school chaplaincy and guidance counselling as well as the establishment of the Institute of Guidance Counsellors, the Irish Association for Pastoral Care in Education (IAPCE) and the School Chaplains Association have contributed greatly to the present situation whereby most second-level teachers in Ireland now recognise pastoral care as a dimension of their professional work.

Despite these developments and the emerging recognition of pastoral care as a dimension of teacher professionalism, there are still differing views on what pastoral care can mean. These perceptions of pastoral care can be generally described in terms of three stages. These stages of pastoral care are intrinsic to the daily endeavours of teachers as professionals in that they are rooted in their professional attitude and personal relationships with their pupils. I describe the first stage as *humanistic* pastoral care, the second as *spiritual* pastoral care, and the third as *curricular* pastoral care. These stages of pastoral care can occur simultaneously or in isolation depending on the pupil's needs and the competence of the teacher.

Humanistic Pastoral Care

In describing this first stage of pastoral care as humanistic I am not inferring anything that could be described as humanism. This stage is concerned with the essentials of life that are a prerequisite of education such as the need for food, the need for warmth, the need for security and a sense of belonging. Teachers will offer this type of pastoral care in the most routine of ways by affirming their pupils when they do well, by making sure that the classroom is a safe and welcoming place and by letting each pupil know that they are interested in them through frequent use of their name and by asking questions about other aspects of their life apart from their academic work. Where it is apparent that a student has specific needs due to a learning difficulty or a disadvantaged background, the teacher might be involved in a more *'reactive'* type of pastoral care such as the running of a breakfast or homework club or liasing with social services. Sometimes a pupil may require a more skilled type of support beyond the competences of their teacher and this is where the teacher will recognise the need to refer the pupil to the guidance counsellor or the school psychologist. However, essentially this humanistic stage of pastoral care requires no more from the teacher than a professional attitude and a genuine interest in the well being of his/her pupils.

Spiritual Pastoral Care

Research and experience has shown that young people do search for meaning and seek to explain their life situations through authentic relationships and spiritual definitions.[32] Consequently, it would not be possible for a teacher to claim to have a personal relationship with their pupils and to ignore the spiritual dimension of their life. In describing this stage of pastoral care as *spiritual* I am not necessarily referring to any one denomination or religious belief system. Although for some, the spiritual and the religious are synonymous, it is important to recognise that they are not always one and the same and that the spiritual dimension of the pupil pre-empts any religious affiliations.[33] In fact the over-association of these two concepts can lead to reluctance on the part of some teachers to see themselves as having a contribution to make to their pupil's spiritual development. However, spirituality is more than membership of a particular religion, which suggests that the teacher's contribution to spiritual development is important if students are to realise their full potential as human beings. Furthermore, spiritual development does not just take place in Religious Education or at assembly. It takes place in every subject and classroom and most importantly it takes place within the personal relationship shared by the teacher with the pupil. There has been a tendency in Irish schools to see the pupil's spiritual development as the responsibility of the religious educator or to identify it solely with sacramental preparation or the transmission of doctrinal information for the churches. In fact this practice goes against the teachings of the Catholic Church itself, which state that this dimension of education is the responsibility of the whole school and not just the religion teacher.[34] Spirituality has been described by Rodger as:

'...not knowing something different, it is a different way of knowing; it is not doing something different, it is a different way of doing; it is not being something different, it is a different way of being.'[35]

Teachers who recognise that pupil's are spiritual beings will seek to promote this spirituality in the way they pace their lessons, and the use of strategies which will allow time and space for prayer, meditation and reflection on the deeper questions which arise during their learning. For example, during a lesson on famines in the Developing World a teacher might not only teach the socio-economic causes of famines, but they might also help students to consider more spiritual questions such as 'why are some people born in these countries and others are not?' 'What is the meaning of suffering?' 'Why do bad things happen to good people?' In the same way that teachers are concerned with a pupil's cognitive development so too are they concerned with other aspects of their development such as the spiritual dimension. In recognising the importance of the spiritual development of the pupils, teachers can be said to be promoting a holistic education in the way that is indicated by the Education Act (1998). Consequently, it can be argued that teacher professionalism in Ireland is holistic in nature in that it embraces the cognitive and spiritual development of the pupil. From time to time a pupil's spiritual needs may require a greater competency than their teacher possess, for example when a pupil experiences bereavement. Again, as a professional the teacher will have the skill to recognise this situation and to refer the pupil onto someone who is more skilled in spirituality such as the school chaplain or a member of the local clergy.

Curricular Pastoral Care

This third stage of pastoral care refers to a teacher's involvement in the many taught pastoral programmes in our schools such as *SPHE, CSPE, RSE* and *RE*. These programmes can be described as *'proactive'* and *'developmental'* in that they seek to develop the pupil's life skills, self esteem and confidence and in doing so prepare the pupil to live a complete and fulfilled life.[36] These programmes have been added to the national curriculum in Ireland over the last number of years and the extent to which they have been implemented varies from school to school. What is clear, though, is that in introducing these programmes to the national curriculum the government has given teachers who are involved in pastoral care an equal status with those who are involved with the more academic subjects. However, there is a risk in establishing pastoral care in the formal curriculum and that is that it may become over-identified with a small number of teachers and a specific place in the timetable. The provision of a pastoral syllabus is important, but it would be wrong if such a syllabus became equated with the totality of pastoral care, which as outlined above is a fundamental dimension to the relationship between the teacher and the pupil, and consequently it is fundamental to teacher professionalism.

Conclusion

Throughout this chapter I have tried to show how teachers can be described as professionals and that the pursuit of the students pastoral needs is a characteristic of this teacher professionalism. However, whether it is correct to describe teachers as pastoral care professionals is another matter. In so far as teachers, who are professionals, care for the well being of their pupils, then it is true to say that teachers are 'caring professionals'. However, to describe a teacher as a 'pastoral care professional' would seem to indicate that the practitioner had a competency or expert knowledge beyond the ordinary competency of a classroom teacher in area such as counselling, psychology and spirituality. Although the Colleges of Education in Ireland give a basic training to teachers at the pre-service stage in philosophy, psychology and sociology, teachers, like doctors and other professionals, cannot be said to possess any great depth of technical expertise in these areas. Consequently, the term 'pastoral care professional' may be better used to describe those who have received a specific training in the discipline of pastoral care such as Guidance Counsellors and School Chaplains.

The teacher–pupil relationship is essential to the professional nature of teaching and the wider school ethos. In this context teachers act out of a genuine concern for the well being of their pupils. However, it is clear that they do not possess the skills or expert knowledge to meet all of their pupils' pastoral needs all of the time and will have to refer to other more qualified practitioners. In other words, while it may not be true to describe teachers as pastoral care professionals, it is true to describe them as caring professionals.

It is clear that teachers' professionalism is closely linked to the ethos of the school. Through the development of a personal integration of values, empathy with pupils and colleagues, vision and adaptability teachers are seen to possess a professional attitude and so enhance the ethos of the school.

Notes

1. Education Act, 1998 (9d).
2. Boldt, S. School *Culture and Ethos* (Dublin, Marino 2000) p. 41.
3. See Irish Times, ASTI Strike Action.
4. Giesecke, H., Das 'Ende der Erziehung'. Ende oder Anfang pädagogischer Professionalität. *Pädagogische Professionalität.* A. Combe and W. Helsper. (Frankfurt: Main, 1999) pp. 391–403.
5. Education Act 1998 (Ireland) Education Act 1988 (England and Wales).
6. Abbott and Wallace, 1990, Freidson, 1994, Hargreaves, 1994, May, 2001.
7. Hargreaves, A., Goodson, I., 'Teachers Professional Lives: aspirations and actualities'in Goodson, I., Hargreaves, A., *Teachers; Professional Lives*, (London: Flamer Press, 1996) p. 1.
8. Sardar, Z. 'Professionals who lost their virtue' in *New Statesman* (10 July 2000) pp. 25–7.
9. Williams, K., 'Professions and Professionalism: The Case of Teaching' in *Issues in Education, ASTI Education Journal*, Vol. 4 (Dublin, Association of Secondary Teachers of Ireland, 2001) p. 23.
10. *Ibid.* p. 24.
11. Gaden, T. G., 'Professional Attitudes' in *Irish Educational Studies*, Vol. 7:1 (Dublin, Educational Studies Association of Ireland, 1988) p. 29.
12. *Ibid.* p. 29.
13. *Ibid.* p. 31.
14. Rogers, K. 'Empathic: an unappreciated way of being' in *The Counselling Psychologist*, Vol. 5 (2) 2. pp. 106–7.
15. Cooper, B., 'Rediscovering the Personal in Education' in Best R., *Education for Spiritual, Moral, Social and Cultural Development* (London, Continuum, 2000) p. 121.
16. Kohlberg 1981; Rogers 1975.
17. Cooper, B., 'Rediscovering the Personal in Education' in Best R., *Education for Spiritual, Moral, Social and Cultural Development* (London, Continuum, 2000) p. 124.
18. Gaden, T.G., 'Professional Attitudes' in *Irish Educational Studies*, Vol. 7:1 (Dublin, Educational Studies Association of Ireland, 1988) p. 32.
19. *Ibid.* p. 32.
20. Watkins and Wagner, 1987.
21. Smyth, A., *Discipline for Learning* (Langford, 1996).
22. *Ethics* II, 1.
23. Best R., 'Pastoral Care in the Millennium' in Collins and McNiff, *Rethinking Pastoral Care* (New York, Routledge, 1999) p. 21.
24. Norman, J., *Pastoral Care in Second Level Schools: The Teacher* (Dublin, CRRE, 2002).
25. Collins, Ú., Mc Niff, J., *Rethinking Pastoral Care* (New York, Routledge, 1999) p. 8.
26. Campbell, A., *Rediscovering Pastoral Care* (London, Darton, Longman and Todd, 1998) p. 31.
27. Lang, P., 'Pastoral Care: Some Reflections and Possible Influences' in *Pastoral Care in Education*, 2:2 (Oxford, Blackwell, 1982) p. 61.
28. Collins, in Lang P., Katz, Y., Menezes, I.(1998) *Affective Education*, (London: Cassell).

29. Education Reform Act, 1988, 1a.
30. Talbot, M., 'Developing SMSC for the Curriculum' in Best, R., *Education for Spiritual, Moral, Social and Cultural Development* (London, Continuum, 2000) p. 13.
31. National Education Convention Secretariat, 1994:53.
32. Tuohy, D., Cairns, P., *Youth 2K, Threat or Promise to a Religious Culture* (Dublin, Marino, 2000) pp. 196-7.
33. Hay, D., Nye, R., *The Spirit of the Child*, (London, Fount, 1998) p. 21*ff.*
34. *Religious Dimension of Education in a Catholic School*, (Vatican,1988) article 64.
35. Rodger, A., 'Human Spirituality: Towards an Educational Rationale' in Best. R., *Education*, Spirituality and the Whole Child, (London, Cassell, 1996) p. 60.
36. Best, R., 'Pastoral Care in the Millennium' in Collins and McNiff, *Rethinking Pastoral Care* (New York, Routledge, 1999) p. 19.

Chapter 6

The Catholic School and the Common Good

It could be said that through maintaining such a strong presence among the better off in society, that some Religious Communities are not only contributing to the growth of a secular and post-modern society but they are actually helping to perpetuate it among future generations.

T HE data available on ethos in Irish Catholic schools raises some very important questions about the purpose of Catholic schools and their role in Irish society. It is clear that there is a strong academic focus in Catholic schools in Ireland, although research in other countries, including the USA, shows that this is not a characteristic reserved to Irish Catholic schools alone.[1] This dimension of ethos in Catholic schools may have arisen out of a historical recognition of education as a key to personal and economic development. However, the Irish Catholic Church's reliance on its role in management to influence the ethos of schools has led to a situation whereby the operative ethos of some Catholic secondary schools is failing to produce young Catholics who are as interested in contributing to the social capital as they are to the economic capital of the country. Research indicates that as a society Irish people appear to be less generous and caring than they were in the past.[2] I will now explore some of these fundamental issues concerning the purpose and role of the Catholic school, which were raised by the data in the previous chapter.

The Purpose of the Catholic School

The purpose of the Catholic school and its role in society is clearly set out in a number of documents that arose out of the Second Vatican Council and to which I have already referred in chapter one. Most notably though, *The Catholic School*[3] and *The Catholic School on the Threshold of the Third Millennium*[4] give us the clearest vision of the nature of Catholic schools. Both of these documents outline the Church's vision of the Catholic school as an enterprise that exists not just for the Church itself but also for the common good. In fact, the first document emphasises the oneness of the schools role in the twofold mission of realising the Churchs' goals and the common good.

> For the Catholic school mutual respect means service to the Person of Christ. Co-operation between brothers and sisters in Christ. A policy of working for the common good is undertaken seriously as working for the building up of the kingdom of God.[5]

The document goes on to reflect on the communitarian nature of the Catholic school:

> Today especially one sees a world which clamours for solidarity and yet experiences the rise of new forms of individualism. Society can take note from the Catholic school that it is possible to create true communities out of a common effort for the common good.[6]

This document also highlights the role of the Catholic school in prioritising the provision of education to the poor and those on the edge of society, warning against the provision of education just for the wealthy and powerful in society.

First and foremost the Church offers its educational service to the poor … Since education is an important means of improving the social and economic condition of the individual and of peoples, if the Catholic school were to turn its attention exclusively or predominantly to those from wealthier social classes it could be contributing towards maintaining their privileged position and could there by continue to favour a society which is unjust.[7]

Fundamentally, *The Catholic School* presents a picture of Catholic education that should be experienced as open, communal and has a particular mission to the poor. When we consider the continued trend in Irish society towards individualism and indifference to religious values we must ask ourselves to what extent are Irish Catholic schools challenging these developments in society. From the research into Irish Catholic secondary schools it seems that rather than promoting community and concern for the poor, many of these schools use practices such as *streaming* which promote individualism and elitism. While there are many Religious Communities who work among the less well off, there are also some Religious Communities in Ireland, such as the Jesuits and the Spiritans, who for the most part have traditionally provided education exclusively for the children of the better off in Irish society. About 50% of the students in single sex voluntary Catholic schools come from middle to upper class backgrounds, compared to about 20% in the vocational schools.[8] It could be said that through maintaining such a strong presence among the better off in society, that some Religious Communities are not only contributing to the growth of a secular and post-modern society but they are actually helping to perpetuate it among future generations.

The promotion of the common good through the Catholic school was stressed again in the most recent document from the Vatican:

The Catholic school's public role is clearly perceived. It has come into being as a private initiative but as an expression of a public character. It fulfils a service of public usefulness and, although clearly and decidedly configured in the perspective of the Catholic faith, is not reserved to Catholics only, but is open to all those who appreciate and share its educational project.[9]

The objections in May 2000 by Dr. Smith, the Bishop of Meath, to the children of parents who do not attend mass and contribute to the parish finances,[10] attending schools in his diocese seems rather inconsistent with the spirit of this statement and the public nature of the Catholic school as specified in the above document. This can give rise to tensions. However, the Bishop's frustration can be understood when we consider that Catholic schools in Ireland have, at a minimum cost to the State, for generations served the educational, social and economic good of the country. The clearest example of how the Catholic Church has served the common good in Ireland can be seen in the role played by Religious Communities in the provision of free education for all. For decades many nuns, brothers and priests returned their teaching salaries back into paying the costs of new buildings to accommodate the increase in the number of students who were availing of the State's policy of free education for all. In this sense it is without doubt a fact that Catholic schools in the past have served the common good in Ireland.

However, during the recession of the 1980s, the relatively small number of places in third-level colleges and the limited availability of work placed undue emphasis on the results accrued by students in their Leaving Certificate and consequently the *'points race'* as we know it began. Over the years schools placed huge emphases on success in the Leaving Certificate as a means of gaining places in college and employment. It is here that we see the genesis of an operational ethos in Catholic schools that saw the expressive goals, such as the development of character, displaced by the instrumental goals such as teaching and learning. This situation was further exacerbated by the Church's over reliance on their role as patron/trustee to influence the ethos of schools.

Characteristics of a Successful Catholic School

In their research in the USA, Bryk, Lee and Holland found that Catholic schools have made a major contribution to the common good of American society, especially where schools were located in disadvantaged urban communities. The authors of this survey identified four basic qualities that they believed made the Catholic school more effective than public schools in terms of their contribution to the common good:

- An emphasis on an academic curriculum for all students.
- A strong sense of community in the school.
- Decentralised management.
- A common sense of purpose among the teachers, which came from their sense of teaching as a vocation.[11]

While many Irish Catholic schools will share some or all of the above qualities, the research as outlined in the previous chapter would seem to suggest that the qualities which make American Catholic schools so effective are just as likely to be found in Ireland in a community school such as Mount Seskin.[12]

Pastoral Care

Like the American teachers,[13] the teachers at Mount Seskin placed the development of character at the centre of the school's mission and the data from students' responses would seem to indicate that the operational ethos of the school reflected this.

Furthermore, Bryk et al. highlighted the role of the school chaplain in promoting the social capital of the school.[14] As an extension of the principal, the chaplain tends to the personal needs of the students and staff as well as the overall character of the school community. Here again we find similarities with the Irish community school model where full-time school chaplains are employed as full members of the community school staff. Research carried out by the Department of Chaplaincy Studies at the Mater Dei Institute of Education, Dublin revealed that chaplains in community schools spend most of their time providing one-to-one counselling, leading liturgy, mediating in discipline problems, and addressing educational disadvantage.[15] In the absence of full-time chaplains in Catholic secondary schools, one wonders who provides this support, if at all. It was assumed to occur via contact with religions and others.

Furthermore, many of the changes that have occurred in Irish society over the past number of years, such as the increase in parental separation and divorce, have resulted in schools taking on a role which goes beyond any narrow definitions of education in terms of academics. Often the school is the first place a student will seek support with a personal problem or difficulty at home. In the future schools will have to become one-stop-shops, offering a wide range of services to meet students pastoral needs in order to support their educational development. Mount Seskin Community School has already made some moves in this direction in the development of its *Integrated Student Support* (ISS) system. At the time of the study, the ISS team consisted of a group of teachers from the special education department in the school, the home-school-community liaison teacher, the guidance counsellor, and local youth workers, the St. Vincent De Paul Society and the public health nurse. The group was chaired and co-ordinated by the school chaplain. The ISS team met once a month to review the progress of the students with the greatest needs and tried to provide follow up support in a confidential and integrated manner.

Counter-Cultural Ethos

Writing on the role of the Catholic school in the UK, Gerald Grace highlights the role of the Catholic school as 'a counter cultural force to strengthen the spiritual and moral culture in society'.[16] In the light of the new more academically focused RE programme in Catholic schools, it is hard to see how these schools will 'strengthen the spiritual and moral culture of society' without full-time pastoral care professionals such as chaplains who will provide students with an experience of faith, not always guaranteed in the RE class. Grace comments on the increased secularisation of society, where:

... the very idea of God is marginalized or entirely removed from consideration and the discourse of the sacred becomes weaker as the discourse of utilitarian concerns (economic planning, bureaucratic requirements, technological innovations, consumer choice) becomes stronger.[17]

When we consider the apparent marginalisation of religion within the curriculum of Catholic schools as reported in the data from McDonnell's research, it seems that Catholic schools in Ireland will have to tend to their own ethos before they can act as a counter cultural force in an increasingly secularised society.

Christian Citizenship Education

Grace goes on to outline the implications of the Church's teaching on the Catholic School and the common good for educational policy and practice. He identifies the need for Catholic schools to be engaged in 'Christian citizenship education'[18] programmes that prepare young people to play an active democratic role in society. The need for Catholic schools in Ireland to provide this type of education is clearly seen in recent years through the low number of people turning out for elections or going forward for important community or political positions. It is hard to see how any school could credibly teach on democracy without examining its own structures and procedures. The relatively small number of schools that have yet to establish student councils or engage parents in the ongoing life of the school is a clear indication of how far the ethos of our Catholic school system has yet to go in terms of modelling democracy for its students.

'Common Good' Awareness

Grace highlights the need for Catholic schools to actively develop what he calls 'common good talents and skills' in their students. He warns that for a school simply to develop the intelligence, talents and skills of young people on an individual basis would result in 'clever but also self-centred and materially acquisitive individuals with no regard for any conception of the common good'.[19] Both McDonnell and O'Keefe concluded in their research studies that Catholic secondary schools in Ireland had become particularly focused on academic achievement resulting in an ethos that could be described as competitive and individualistic. It seems that these Catholic schools will have to find new methods if they are to develop an ethos which equally promotes the development of students intelligence and skills alongside a religious and moral understanding that their personal abilities should be used for the benefit of others.

Student leadership programmes such as the *Meitheal* programme in the Kildare and Leighlin Diocese and the *Gluais* programme in the Archdiocese of Dublin have been developed to help young people gain an experience of putting their gifts to use for the benefit of other members of the school and the wider community.[20] There is a real need for programmes like these to be recognised as part of the formal activities of a school by allowing more time and for students to be able to acquire credits for their participation in such programmes which could be used to support their application for some third-level courses.

Celebrating Achievements of All

One of the easiest ways to quickly assess the ethos of a school is to take a walk around the building and to note what kind of trophies and photographs make their way onto the walls of honour along its hallways. These trophies clearly indicate what kind of achievement is valued in the school. If a school is to truly develop the gifts and talents of all of its students, it must acknowledge in a public way every kind of talent and achievement and not confine its forms of public recognition to the spheres of academia and sports. In one school I know of, a student who had not achieved particularly high marks in the academic area, won a national Irish dancing competition outside the school, yet at the end of the year, his achievement was excluded from being mentioned at prize-giving because the principal believed that to mention this achievement would cause him to be ridiculed by the other students. On the other hand, to mention it, among a number of other achievements by several students, would have said a lot about what the school valued. In another school, a final year student gained his full licence after passing his driving test, something that is unusual for a seventeen year old first time round. Again, at prize giving this achievement received no formal recognition. If Catholic schools are to live up to the holistic and Christian aims of their mission statements they will have to provide forms of public recognition for all kinds of contributions and achievements by students.

Positive Discipline

Owing to the many sociological and cultural changes in Ireland, students in schools today often come from homes where that which is valued differs considerably from the culture of the school, resulting in a clash between the culture of the school and the dominant culture of the home that can manifest itself at times in student indiscipline and disruption in the classroom.[21] Catholic schools today are facing new discipline problems and levels of student non-compliance that would have been unheard of in the past. Perhaps more than anything else, procedures for discipline provide the clearest indication of ethos in a Catholic school.

Where schools have been successful in dealing with problems of discipline there has been a high level of teacher collaboration in terms of implementing policies and procedures which are aimed at motivating students to do well while at the same time reduce levels of disruption in the classroom. In a Catholic school, discipline policies and procedures should not contribute to a punitive ethos but rather focus on the development of character. Discipline should be an aspect of the student's development rather than a controlling force based on an imbalance of power.

In an attempt to deal with student misbehaviour many Catholic schools have adopted a so-called positive discipline programme called *'Discipline for Learning'* (DFL).[22] DFL is rooted in the behaviourist approach to learning and relies on extrinsic methodologies to promote learning. Usually DFL employs a tariff system that involves an incremental taxonomy of sanctions and rewards. When the rules are obeyed rewards are given. When they are disobeyed sanctions are applied. The key to the effectiveness of this programme is its uniformity: all teachers must adhere to the system of rewards and sanctions, so students learn to know what is expected of them at all times. While some aspects of this programme are useful for teachers in schools, the programme in its purest form fails to treat the students as individuals and take account of background factors that may affect student behaviour.[23] Such a taxonomy contradicts an ethos that aims to meet individual needs.[24] In so far as DFL fails to take account of the individual student's needs, it is unchristian and has no place in a Catholic school.

It is essential that the teachers in a Catholic school continuously model respectful behaviour with each other and their students. This is affirmed by the Martin Report, which recommends that selection procedures for entry into the teaching profession should take into account the importance of the teacher as a role model in the lives of the students.[25] Catholic schools in particular must be attentive to the ability of their teachers to model Christian behaviour and to promote it among their students.

The discipline policy in a Catholic school should always serve the development of the students' character. It will be positive and proactive in that it should anticipate students' needs before they arise and seek to help the individual student to achieve their best. The discipline policy should form part of the school's pastoral care programme and should involve as much support procedures as it does sanctions. If a school starts with a student's needs, the discipline policy will be built around them, whereas if a school starts with an arbitrary code of conduct, the student will not benefit.

The data from Mount Seskin Community School indicates that the community school model produces an ethos where the integration of the student's personal, social and religious development can be achieved in a way that is not being fully realised in Catholic secondary schools such as the ones studied by

McDonnell and by O'Keefe and referred to in the research by Fulton. Findings such as these present the Irish Catholic Church with a dilemma in terms of its traditional presence in education. As seen in chapter two, for the most part, in its desire to influence the ethos of schools, the Catholic Church in Ireland has relied primarily on its role as school patron or trustee. It now seems that this somewhat paternalistic presence in Catholic schools has not been as successful as the institutional Church's more pastoral presence in the community school sector, particularly in terms of achieving the educational goals outlined in the post-conciliar documents, such as the development of the whole human person[26] and the integration of faith, life and culture.[27]

The most recent document on education from the Church articulates an understanding of school ethos that is deeply rooted in the ongoing life of the school. The document states that the school ethos:

> ... is constituted by the interaction and collaboration of its various components: students, parents, teachers, directors and non-teaching staff. Attention is rightly given to the importance of the relations existing among all those who make up the educating community.[28]

In emphasising the important contribution of habitual relations to the Catholic school's ethos, this document brings together the Catholic Church's vision of educational ethos since the Second Vatican Council. As with Aristotle in his *Ethics* (Book II), ethos for the post-conciliar Church is concerned with the development of the whole person arising out of the dynamic of relationships that are at the heart of the habitual life of the school community. Thus in the above document, the Catholic Church continues to highlight the necessity to develop an experience of Christian community in the Catholic school and identifies the teachers and parents as having the "prime responsibility for creating this unique Christian climate".[29] The research carried out at Mount Seskin indicates that the developing of a community spirit and the common good at the school is a priority for parents who identified the personal and social development of the students as the chief aims of the school.

In short, the community school can be described as an effective *de facto* Catholic school in that it possesses several characteristics that reflect the current vision of the Catholic Church in terms of a successful Catholic school. Not only is the community school focused on the personal needs of the individual students[30] but also through its various academic and pastoral programmes it is actively cultivating a relatively high degree of integration between the students' personal, social and to a lesser degree religious development.[31] Furthermore, in the case of the community school, the expectations of the students, teachers and parents in terms of the goals of the school have fostered an ethos in which students are educated through interpersonal relationships, thus producing a strong community dimension to the school's operative ethos.[32]

Implications for the future of the Catholic School

Reflection

For about two hundred years Catholic schools, as we know them, have existed in Ireland. Throughout this time, these schools have not only served as a means of perpetuating the Catholic faith but they have also served the common good at times when most of the people were poor with few educational possibilities. It is now time for the Religious Communities who have provided these schools to continue their reflection on their traditional role as managers in education and ask themselves if this type of presence in education will a) best serve their mission as a Religious Community and b) serve the common good of a society which is becoming more and more removed from religious points of reference. CORI has acknowledged that the time may have come for Religious to hand over the trusteeship of their schools to the laity of the Church.[33] While in the past the Religious have played a huge role in the development of the Irish education system, the time has come for them to discern the needs of contemporary society and find ways of meeting these needs.

National Policy

On the other hand, handing over the trusteeship of schools should not be perceived as a total withdrawal from education. As a result of the huge involvement of Religious Communities in education over the past two hundred or so years, the Religious have developed a considerable amount of experience in the management of schools and consequently have a responsibility to use this experience for the common good. Through CORI the Religious have become more influential in terms of national educational policy. This is a form of 'proactive' leadership that Religious are committed to continuing in the future.[34] Through CORI Religious can bring their unique vision of education into dialogue with policy makers at government level and consequently influence the wider ethos of Irish education in the future.

Seek out the Poor

The Catholic schools of the future will have to have a strong association with the poor and the vulnerable in society. Most Religious Communities' involvement in schools began with a concern for the poor.[35] While some have remained faithful to their founding trust, others have a less direct involvement with the marginalized at this stage. As mentioned previously, the majority of young people in Catholic schools in Ireland come from the better-off sections of society. While many of these schools will continue to exist, the measure of their success will be closely linked to their ability to bring the members of their school community into contact with the reality of the issues facing the poor and vulnerable in our society. This aspect of education in a Catholic school will particularly be based on the RE and CSPE/ SPHE programmes. It is, however, also important for the school to provide experiences for their students that will help them to meet and experience the world of the less well-off. This will be achieved through student exchanges, visits, fund-raising and sponsored fasts.

At a more fundamental level, Catholic schools in the future will have to examine their selection processes at entry level and explore the reasons for their traditional intake. For example, a Catholic school can claim a concern for the poor in society when its students are driven to school in large cars from all parts of the suburbs, and the local children make do with gazing through the gates at their better-off peers. I would go as far as to say that for Religious Communities to be faithful to their original trust they may need to consider the location of their schools today. While they probably started out in response to a need for education in a particular area, maybe the time has come for them to seek out new areas where the need is greater. Otherwise they run the risk of becoming over-associated with the better-off classes that they are now catering for.

Pastoral Presence

Furthermore, it would seem that in a society which is becoming increasingly secular that the Church needs to find ways of creating new and meaningful religious points of reference as a means of contact for people with the institutional Church. Traditionally, contact with the Church came in the celebration of the sacraments, which depended on a way of life that was fundamentally communal and centred around the parish. The Church could rely on the structures of society reinforcing this way of life. Today, particularly in urban areas, as a consequence of employment and housing costs, people often live in satellite towns from which they commute to work and return again late in the evening and maybe totally vacate at weekends. Consequently their lives have become less connected to the place in which they live. Instead, many Irish people today find community in their place of work or study, in a gymnasium or supermarket. Some even search for community in the virtual world of the Internet. Consequently, the Catholic Church is faced with developing new points of reference through which young people today can develop their faith.

The Catholic school is no exception, in a post-modern Irish

society where almost 60% of households have two parents working outside the home and with parental separation 135% higher than it was in the early 1980s,[36] the school takes on the role of providing a primary experience of community and even family for young people. In searching for a new way to reach this generation, I suggest that the Church needs to return to its roots and move away from control and management towards a more pastoral role in Irish schools. The success of the role of the chaplain in the community school has been referred to earlier. Over 90% of teachers in post-primary schools in Ireland claim that their initial pre-service training was inadequate in terms of preparing them to meet students pastoral needs.[37] Furthermore, in Boldt's study into ethos in Irish schools he found that teachers spent most of their time encouraging academic development despite an awareness of student's pastoral needs.[38]

While it will always be necessary for Catholic schools to maintain high academic standards, it is clear that in order for the Church to realise the holistic aims of the Vatican documents on education, a lot more energy and resources will have to be dedicated to developing a pastoral ethos in Catholic schools. School principals will have to allow more space on timetables for subjects that focus primarily on the development of the person as well as allowing time for in-service training for staff in this area. Each school should have an oratory or prayer room that is attractively laid out and centrally located where students, parents and staff can drop in during a busy school day.

It is important to note that a concern for the pastoral dimension of education does not imply that a school decreases its expectations in the academic areas. It is absolutely true that the most fundamental function of a school is to promote learning and that the principal job of a teacher is to teach. However, the students learn better when they feel that the teacher is interested in them an individuals. At the same time, not every teacher has to be a counsellor or a chaplain. Apart from the fact that not all teachers will have the interest, expertise or suitability to offer this kind of support to students, teachers should spend the majority of their time teaching. On the other hand, if we consider the holistic aims of the Education Act[39] as well as Vatican documents such as *The Catholic School on the Threshold of the Third Millennium*, it is clear that schools have a responsibility to cater for the personal and spiritual needs of students. Consequently, all Catholic schools should have two equally important arms, academic and pastoral. In the same way that a school will seek to employ the best and most professional teachers, it should also employ those who are professionally trained in pastoral care. Pastoral care is not about being 'nice' or a 'soft' option. Pastoral care in a school recognises the totality of the student's life and is concerned with supporting students in areas of their life that may hinder their ability to achieve in education. It seeks to offer them the space and time needed to deal with problems such as death, separation or divorce, low self-esteem, depression, loneliness, bullying and illness. Pastoral care is not only concerned with the problems that students experience, it is also concerned with providing students with opportunities to develop a sense of belonging and purpose in life and to consider their spiritual journey. Through the work of counsellors, chaplains and support workers the ordinary subject teacher is freed up to pursue their primary concern, which must be the teaching of a curriculum. Pastoral care is part of good education, good education involves good teaching and hence both pastoral care and teaching are important elements of a Catholic school.

If ethos has to do with the development of character, then it is only right that schools should pay attention to students' personal needs as well as their academic needs. In the future, the effectiveness of Catholic schools will be measured by their ability to develop an ethos in which students can learn while at the same time be cared for.

Organisation of Learning

Within many Catholic schools in Ireland, partly due to the large numbers seeking secondary education, a number of processes for the organisation of learning based on student ability have emerged. *Streaming* is a system of classroom organisation in which students are grouped according to fixed criteria such as their general ability in a subject such as mathematics or English. Although the state curriculum does not allow for this at primary level, teachers (as a means of allocating work and monitoring progress) can often use it within their class. At secondary level, about 70% of Irish schools use some form of streaming to separate students of different abilities.[40] There has been very little analysis of the effects of streaming on students. Those who advocate streaming claim that it benefits students because it is egalitarian in that it serves the interest of all students; it eliminates competition between students of different abilities and so is good for self-esteem not to mention that it helps the teacher to assign work set at a common level for a particular ability group.

On the other hand there has been very little analysis of the effects of streaming on students in Irish schools apart from the research carried out by Hannan and Boyle in 1987 and by Lynch in 1989. Both of these studies identified some problems regarding streaming in relation to the negative impact on 'lower' streamed students.

Without entering into a full analysis of this process here, it is enough for us to consider the place of such a process in the light of the Catholic school and its common good mission. Any method for the organisation of learning in a Catholic school must be analysed in the light of the school's holistic and communitarian understanding of education as outlined in a recent document on education from the Catholic Bishops of England and Wales:

> Every member of a school community possesses a basic dignity that comes from God and is therefore worthy of respect...the Church's social vision should likewise be evident in the organisation and management of the class-room and in the relationships between and among staff.[41]

It would seem to me that streaming organises students into different ability groupings on the basis of one or two very narrow variables. Consequently, students' intelligence is being assessed in a way that ignores the totality of the individual. Secondly, any teaching method that ignores the needs of individuals fails in terms of the Catholic school's aim of developing the whole person. Thirdly, streaming has been found to create social ghettoes in that students tend not to mix outside their own ability grouping.[42] This in turn leads to the formation of sub-cultures that can undermine the communitarian nature of ethos in a Catholic school. Finally, streaming can lead to an ethos that is competitive, hierarchical and elitist. The Catholic school should be seeking to challenge these aspects of society not employ organisational processes which contribute to them. The alternative to streaming is mixed-ability grouping. This has huge consequences in terms of allocation of teachers and resources. In terms of the Catholic school, it would be more appropriate to use a method of grouping that allows students to develop many kinds of intelligences while at the same time developing their social abilities. This in turn will have a positive effect on society and the common good. The Catholic school must seek to use methods of organisation of learning that are open, communitarian and that have a particular concern for the weaker members of the school community. It is clear that streaming through its emphases on academic scores and the separation of students of different abilities undermines the holistic and communitarian character of ethos in a Catholic school.

Life-long Learning

There is a tendency to view education in terms of the formal curriculum for primary and secondary school. However, education is a life-long process and in terms of the common good, individual Catholic schools can make a significant contribution to the ongoing education of the local community. Catholic schools all over Ireland are in a unique position to support local development through the concept of life-long learning. The school recognising its unique role in the local community can facilitate members of the community in discerning their own individual and community needs through guidance and information. Some Catholic schools have already appointed Guidance and Information officers who are responsible for supporting the life-long learning of parents, teachers and students as well as the wider local community. The Catholic school has a responsibility to the wider community beyond its gates and this can be achieved through making the premises available to local community groups for meetings and courses. Through developing an ethos of life-long learning among the school community, the Catholic school will serve the common good of the local and wider community.

Community Network of Schools

One of the interesting observations of life at Mount Seskin Community School was the amount of networking that members of the staff were involved in. I have already outlined the Integrated Support System that brought together teachers with local support services. However, there were many other examples of networking which involved staff, parents and students working as part of small, dedicated clusters that were formed among local schools. The school chaplain belonged to a cluster group of local school chaplains who came together about once per month. The home-school-community liaison teacher belonged to a network, as did the guidance counsellor. Staff at the school identified these clusters as being of benefit to themselves professionally and the wider school community. They said that networking was beneficial in terms of:

- Sharing resources and 'best-practice'
- Identifying their own training needs
- Collaborating on projects of mutual benefit to schools
- Making submissions for funding and policy

Gerald Grace points out that the 'realisation of notions of the common good in educational practice seems to imply that a group of Catholic schools in a given locality will want to act as a supportive community network of Catholic schools and not simply as a number of individual and competitive units.'[43] Such networking can benefit individual schools at many levels such as staff recruitment, sharing of resources, partnership planning, helping schools with particular needs and so on. Through this type of partnership Catholic schools not only strengthen each other but also the wider common good as an example of democracy in action. Furthermore, such co-operation will work to break down social and class boundaries between schools and areas.

Conclusion and Analysis

From the *Declaration on Christian Education* (1965) right up to the latest document on education, *The Catholic School on the Threshold of the Third Millennium* (1998), the Catholic Church has recognised that young people are above all educated through relationships.[44] In his research McDonnell found that students in the Catholic secondary schools, particularly single sex boys' schools, did not see the school structures as friendly or caring when they were in need of pastoral care.[45] On the other hand, the students in the community school declared a very high satisfaction rating (80.25%) with the pastoral care programme in their school. Despite the pastoral imperative included in the Education Act (1998)[46] many Catholic secondary schools have yet to implement a full pastoral care plan. It seems that this dimension of education is something that is presumed to be part of the Catholic school and yet the research indicates that it is in this very area that these schools are lacking.

Regarding Religious Education (RE), it seems that in both the community school and the Catholic voluntary schools, this dimension of education has to an extent become marginalized from the rest of the school curriculum, although the students in the community school did seem to have a higher regard for RE (11%) than their counterparts in the Catholic voluntary schools (0.9%). This marginalisation of religion within the school has mainly come about as a result of the conflict between the instrumental and expressive goals of the school and is manifested in the growing reluctance of teachers to effect any kind of dialogue between religious values and the values being mediated through other subjects on the curriculum. As previously mentioned, one of the key concepts in the Catholic Church's understanding of education is the achievement of an integration of faith and culture.[47] If this integration is to be achieved in the Catholic school (voluntary or community) the whole school staff with the parents will have to work together in such a way that students are encouraged to interpret their contemporary experiences in the light of their religious tradition. This will only be possible if RE departments are provided with qualified staff and adequate resources. The researcher at the community school observed several initiatives such as the *Faith Friends* programme which was introduced by the RE teachers and chaplain to help the students to make a connection between the values of RE ad the wider curriculum. These initiatives may account for the higher ranking given to RE by the students in the community school. The recent Education Act (1998) offers a structure that supports the development of a comprehensive RE programme in schools. In its advocacy of the holistic development of the pupil it gives special place to the spiritual and moral formation and, in doing so, mirrors the educational goals of the Catholic school as seen in the Vatican documents.[48]

In the second chapter of this book attention was drawn to the way in which Irish society has changed in recent years. Ireland is increasingly becoming a more secular state with a plurality of beliefs, practices and expectations. At the same time Church practice is decreasing and there are many levels of self-understanding for those who remain committed to the Catholic faith. Increasingly, the idea of the Catholic Church's role as patron or trustee of so many second level schools is becoming increasingly difficult to sustain. In many ways Catholic voluntary secondary schools in Ireland are working out of a model of the Catholic school that is anachronistic, in that it presumes an acceptance by all those in the school community of the religious goals of the school. In fact, Catholic schools are increasingly finding themselves accepting students whose parents either have little or no commitment to the Catholic faith. In the same way that Irish society is changing, so also is the teaching profession. In his research, McDonnell found that only 30% of the teachers in the Catholic secondary schools that he studied believed that the

Catholic Church was offering any kind of inspirational leadership. It must be born in mind that, for the most part, the future of Catholic schools will be in the hands of these lay teachers. In the longer term it is hard to see how these teachers will continue to offer high levels of compliance when they have such low levels of confidence in the institutional Church itself.

Despite the obvious problems that lie ahead for it, the Catholic Church in Ireland is still as committed as it has been in the past to its involvement in education. In the most recent documents from the Vatican, the Church reaffirms its educational goals as the development of the whole human person through an integration of faith, culture and life.[49] The data from Mount Seskin Community School reveal a positive picture in terms of the ability of the community school model to achieve the goals of the Catholic Church where education is concerned. While this study was carried out in just one community school, there is no reason to say that other community schools would not be equally successful in achieving the Church's educational mission. As outlined in Chapter three, for the Church the essential difference between its traditional managerial involvement in voluntary schools and its managerial involvement in the community school, is that the Church as an institution has a minority interest in the management of the community school. More importantly however, the focus of the Church's involvement in the community school is on the ground, working among the students, teachers and parents and so influencing the ongoing life of the school. In the case of the community school, the Church's influence on ethos arises from its involvement within the school community, rather than from a more removed managerial position.

Ultimately, the research data from Mount Seskin, when compared with the data from the other studies, indicate that the ethos of the community school is not so much less academic but more pastoral in nature. If the positive picture presented of ethos at Mount Seskin Community School is typical of other community schools, than there is reason to suggest that the Church could equally achieve its educational aims through increasing its involvement with community schools rather than maintaining lay-run voluntary schools in the future.

Notes

1. Bryk, A., et al., *Catholic Schools and the Common Good*, (Cambridge, Harvard Press, 1993) p. 75.
2. 'MRBI 2001 Survey', quoted in Jones, J., *In Your Opinion, Political & Social Trends in Ireland*, (Dublin, TownHouse, 2001) p. 290.
3. 1977.
4. 1998.
5. *The Catholic School* (1977) Article 60.
6. *Ibid.* Article 62.
7. *Ibid.* Article 58.
8. CORI, *Religious Congregations in Irish Education, A role for the Future*, (Dublin, CORI, November 1997) p. 30.
9. *The Catholic School on the Threshold of the Third Millennium*, (1998) Article 16.
10. The Irish Catholic, May 2000.
11. Bryk, A., et al., *The Catholic School and the Common Good*, (Cambridge, Harvard Press, 1993) pp. 132–4, 150, 142.
12. It is important to acknowledge the role of the community colleges which are part of the VEC sector and for the most part operate in similar terms to the community school except that in a community college the board of management is a sub-committee of the county VEC.
13. Bryk et al., (1993). p. 133.
14. *Ibid.* pp. 140–1.
15. Norman, J., Pastoral Care, School Chaplaincy and Educational Disadvantage, Paper presented to the ESAI Conference, September 2001.
16. Grace, G. *Catholic Schools and the Common Good, What this Means in Educational Practice*, (London, Institute of Education, 2000) p. 7.
17. *Ibid.*
18. *Ibid.* p. 6.
19. *Ibid.*
20. Both of these programmes involve senior students acting as mentors to junior students on an individual and class group basis. As part of their training the students are helped to reflect on their gifts and talents and on how they can best use them for the good of others. See Dolan, R. *Student Leadership Programmes* (NUIM, unpublished M.Ed. thesis, 2001).
21. Martin, M. *Discipline in Irish Schools, Report to the Minister for Education*, (Dublin, 1997) p. 13.
22. Smyth, Adrian, *Discipline for Learning*, (London, 1996).
23. Martin M., (1997) p. 11.
24. O'Brien, T., Promoting Positive Behaviour, (London, Fulton, 1998) p. 99.
25. Martin, M., (1997) p. 61.
26. *Declaration on Christian Education*, (1965) Article 2.
27. *Religious Dimension of Education in a Christian School*, (1988) Article 51.
28. *The Catholic School on the Threshold of the Third Millennium*, (1998) Article 18.
29. *Ibid.* Article 12, 19–20.
30. *Ibid.* Article 9.
31. *Ibid.* Article 14.

32. *Ibid.* Article 18.

33. CORI, (1997) p. 9.

34. McCormack, T., Future Directions for Trusteeship in Furlong, C., Monahan, L., *School Culture ad Ethos,* (Dublin, Marino, 2000) p. 158.

35. CORI, *Religious Congregations in Irish Education, A role for the Future,* (Dublin, CORI, November 1997) p. 13.

36. Central Statistics Office, (Cork, 2000).

37. Norman, J., (2001).

38. Boldt, S., A Vantage Point of Values, in *School Culture and Ethos,* (Dublin, Marino, 2000) p. 41.

39. Education Act, (1998), Section 9 (d).

40. Lynch K., *Equality In Irish Schools,* (Dublin, Gill and Macmillan, 1989).

41. The Catholic Bishops of England and Wales, *The Common Good in Education,* (London, Catholic Education Service, 1997) p. 7.

42. Hargreaves, 1985.

43. Grace, G., (2000) p. 8.

44. *The Catholic School on the Threshold of the Third Millennium* (1998) Article 18.

45. McDonnell, (1995) Vol. II, p. 521.

46. Education Act, (1998) Section 9(d).

47. *Catholic School on the Threshold* (1998) Article 14.

48. *Ibid.* Article 11.

49. *Ibid.* Articles 9, 11.

Reflections on the
Catholic School

Are the resources of spiritual capital among Irish school leaders and teachers being effectively renewed to meet the challenges of a more secular and questioning society?

I READ the draft of James Norman's book shortly after I had completed two research-based studies of Catholic education. The first is a book based upon an investigation of leadership challenges for the head teachers of 60 Catholic secondary schools in London, Liverpool and Birmingham.[1] The second is a chapter for the forthcoming *International Handbook of Educational Leadership and Administration*[2] in which I have raised the issue of mission integrity as a central concern for Catholic schools internationally. There is a substantial measure of agreement between James Norman's research findings and my own, although there are differences in methodology, analysis and argument in our various studies.

On my reading of this book, James Norman has performed a valuable service for Catholic secondary schooling in Ireland.

He has, in effect, constructed an *Agenda for the Mission Review of Catholic schooling in Ireland*, which arises from his review of existing scholarly sources and from his own fieldwork research. This Agenda consists of five key issues, which can best be summarised as follows:

Awareness of Mission Distortion and Individualisation

Irish Catholic secondary schools have, in general, a strong academic profile, which is known and appreciated by parents and students. In this they are clearly serving Irish youth in the realisation of intellectual potential and the effective use of talents. However, as James Norman demonstrates, this very academic success profile generates, ironically, some potential problems for schools which have a distinctive Catholic mission in education. The first problem can be called *mission distortion*. In this case, the academic success culture of a school and its constant enhancement in a competitive world comes to dominate all other objectives and commitments of the educational process. The visible and measurable outcomes of schooling, especially in examination and test results, become more and more important to the detriment of other outcomes.

In this situation, attention and time given to spiritual and moral formation, to personal and social development and the renewal of Catholicity itself may gradually become marginalised. What should be only one part (albeit an important one) of the mission threatens to distort a balanced and Catholic matrix of educational objectives. Frequently connected with this phenomenon is the *individualisation* of the academic mission. The traditional Catholic formula has been 'development of knowledge and skills + spiritual, religious and common good commitments to service = the good Catholic person and citizen'. Contemporary cultural developments in many societies with greater emphasis upon consumerism and individualism threaten that crucial relationship. In an increasing number of schools academic success is becoming an end in itself, a commodity to be acquired and a fulfilment of self without the necessary Catholic and Christian relation to ideas of service. James Norman's research does not establish that these problems are now general in Irish Catholic secondary education because his evidence samples are relatively small. However, his research is indicative of emergent problems and it highlights the need for every Catholic school to engage in self-review of its current ethos and practice.

Monitoring Mission Integrity

My definition of mission integrity is 'fidelity in practice and not just in public rhetoric, to the distinctive and authentic principles of a Catholic education'. These principles include a priority status for spiritual, religious and moral formation and, in the words of the Sacred Congregation for Catholic Education (1977) a service 'to the poor, or those who are deprived of family help and affection, or those who are far from the faith'.[3]

While James Norman does not use directly the language of mission integrity, what emerge from this study are substantive issues related to the mission integrity of Catholic schools in Ireland. For instance, does religious, moral and social formation receive the priority to be expected in a Catholic school? Are Catholic secondary schools clearly in the service of the economic poor, the family support poor and the faith poor in Irish society? The work of James Norman alerts the school leadership (of bishops, patrons/trustees, religious orders and school principals) to their responsibilities to be active guardians of the mission integrity of Catholic education. Is the mission lived and experienced by teachers and students or does it exist only in the formal principles of the schools' mission statements or its prospectus?

Writing about the changing situation of Catholic schools in the USA, Wallace has argued:

> 'There is a major identity crisis occurring in Catholic schools. The dramatic shift from religious to lay personnel raises the question of whether or not some Catholic schools are becoming private schools with a religious memory but secular presence.'[4]

Mission integrity is a central issue for contemporary Catholic education in all societies.

Renewing Spiritual Capital

By spiritual capital I mean 'resources of faith and values devised from commitment to a religious tradition'. Bryk has written about the importance of an inspirational ideology in Catholic schools in the USA and my own research refers to the significance of 'dynamic spiritual capital' in Catholic schools in England. Catholic school leadership in both countries has been powered by the resources of faith and service embodied in its religious and lay leadership. Such leadership was however formed and shaped in the particular circumstances of the past. The crucial question raised by James Norman articulates with other studies. Are the resources of spiritual capital among Irish school leaders and teachers being effectively renewed to meet the challenges of a more secular and questioning society? Unless the spiritual resources of Catholic schooling are being renewed in various ways, then the implication of James Norman's argument, i.e. that of growing secularisation within the schools themselves, will occur.

Listening to the Voice and Experience of the Students

In seeking to understand the ethos of Mount Seskin Community School, James Norman listened seriously to the voice and experience of the students. This is the way forward for all schools, including Catholic schools. The students can tell us about the reality of school ethos as opposed to its formality. They can tell us to what extent a school is meeting their religious, spiritual and social needs as well as their academic expectations. This book should encourage all schools to have the courage to submit themselves to serious evaluation by their own students.

School Chaplains as Agents of Spiritual Renewal

I strongly support James Norman's argument that every Catholic second level school should have the service of chaplains (clerical and lay). In a research study completed in 2001, I analysed the culture and performance of St. Michael's Catholic Comprehensive School, Billingham as it had developed from an earlier study in 1995.[5] I found, against expectation, that the spiritual and religious culture of the school was stronger in 2001 than it had appeared to be in 1995. A major factor in this transformation (attested to by the head teacher and teachers) has been the appointment of two part-time lay chaplains (both women). The Vice-Chair of the Governing Body, a priest, argued that the enhancement of the spiritual culture of the school was very evident and owed much to the activities of the lay chaplains.

If Irish Catholic secondary schools use James Norman's book as the basis for mission renewal and institutional review I am confident that they will reap many benefits.

Professor Gerald Grace
*Director, Centre for Research and Development
in Catholic Education (CRDCE),
University of London Institute of Education*

Notes

1. Grace, G: *Catholic Schools: Mission, Markets and Morality*, London, Routledge Falmer 2002.
2. Grace, G: 'Mission Integrity: Contemporary Challenges for Catholic School Leaders' in *International Handbook of Educational Leadership and Administration*, Dordrecht, Kluwer Academic Press, 2002.
3. Sacred Congregation for Catholic Education: *The Catholic School*, Rome 1977.
4. Wallace, T: 'We are Called: the Principal as Faith Leader in the Catholic School' in Hunt Tetal (Eds.) *Catholic School Leadership*, London, Falmer Press, 2000, p. 191.
5. Grace, G: 'St. Michael's Roman Catholic Comprehensive School' in Maden, M (Ed) *Success Against the Odds: Five Years On*, London, RoutledgeFalmer, 2001.

Bibliography

Aristotle, *Nicomachean Ethics* translated by J.A.K. Thompson (1976) revised by H. Trendennick with an introduction by J. Barnes (London: Penguin).

Barber, N. (1989) *Comprehensive Schooling in Ireland*, (Dublin, ESRI).

Beck, J. (1998) *Morality and Citizenship in Education*, (London, Cassell.

Bernstein, B.(1975) *Class, Codes and Control*, Volume II, (London, Routledge).

Best, R. (1999) 'Pastoral Care and the Millennium' in *Rethinking Pastoral Care*, (New York: Routledge).

Boldt, S., 'A Vantage Point of Values – Findings from School Culture and Ethos Questionnaires' in Furlong, C., Monahan, L., *School Culture and Ethos* (Dublin, Marino, 2000).

Bryk, A., Lee, V., Holland, P., *Catholic Schools and the Common Good*, (Cambridge, MA., Harvard University Press, 1993).

Bunreacht na hÉireann, The Constitution of Ireland, (Dublin, Government Publications, 1938).

Burnett, J. (1967) *Aristotle on Education*, (Cambridge: Cambridge University Press).

Campbell, A. (2000) *Rediscovering Pastoral Care*, (London: Darton, Longman & Todd).

Charting Our Education Future: White Paper on Education (1995) (Dublin: Government of Ireland).

Clancy, P., Drudy, S., Lynch, K., O'Dowd, L., *Irish Society: Sociological Perspectives*, (Dublin, IPA, 1995).

Coleman, J., *High School Achievement, Catholic and Public Schools Compared*, (Chicago, University of Chicago Press, 1982).

Collins, Ú., McNiff, J. (1999) *Rethinking Pastoral Care*, (New York: Routledge).

Conference of Religious in Ireland, *Education Bill 1997, An Analysis*, (Dublin, 1997).

Conference of Religious in Ireland, *Religious Congregations in Irish Education*, (Dublin, 1997).

Conference of Religious in Ireland, *The Future of Trusteeship: A Review of some questions for the way forward*, (Dublin, 1997).

Conference of Religious in Ireland, *The Points System, An Analysis and Review of Some Alternatives*, (Dublin, 1998).

Conference of Religious of Ireland, The Catholic School in Contemporary Society (Dublin, 1991).

Congregation for Catholic Education, *Declaration on Christian Education*, (1965), in the Documents of the Second Vatican Council, ed. Flannery, (Dublin, Dominican Publications, 1981).

Congregation for Catholic Education, *The Catholic School on the Threshold of the Third Millennium*, (Rome, 1998).

Congregation for Catholic Education, *The Catholic School*, (Rome, 1977).

Congregation for Catholic Education, *The Religious Dimension of Education in a Catholic School* (Rome, 1988).

Coolahan, J., *Irish Education: History ad Structure*, (Dublin, IPA, 1981).

Coolahan, J., *Report on the National Education Convention*, (Dublin, Government Publications, 1994).

Cooper, B.(2000) 'Rediscovering the Personal in Education' in Best, R., *Education for Spiritual, Moral, Social and Cultural Development*, (London: Continuum).

Department of Education and Science, *The Primary Curriculum: Introduction* (Dublin, The Stationery Office, 1999).

Devitt, P., *That You May Believe*, (Dublin, Dominican Publications, 1992).

Devitt, P., *Willingly to School*, (Dublin, Veritas, 2000).

Dolan, R., *Student Leadership Programmes*, (Dublin, NUIM Unpublished M.Ed. Thesis, 2001).

Donnelly, C., 'In Pursuit of Ethos', in *British Journal of Education*, (London, June 2000).

Drudy, S., Lynch, K., *Schools and Society in Ireland*, (Dublin, Gill and MacMillan, 1993).

Dunne, J., 'TBA' in Hogan, P., *Partnership and the Benefits of Learning, Symposium*, (Maynooth, ESAI, 1995).

Education Act (1998) (Dublin: Government of Ireland).

Feheney, M., *From Ideal to Action, The Inner Nature of a Catholic School Today*, (Dublin, Veritas, 1998).

Flynn, M., *Catholic Schools and the Communication of Faith*, (New South Wales, St. Paul Publications, 1979).

Fulton, J., ed., *Young Catholics At the New Millennium*, (Dublin, UCD Press, 2000).

Furlong, C., Monahan, L., *School Culture and Ethos, Cracking the Code*, (Dublin, Marino, 2000).

Gaden, T.G. (1988) 'Professional Attitudes' in *Irish Educational Studies*, Vol. 7:1 (Dublin: Educational Studies Association of Ireland).

Gibbon, M., *The Pupil* (Dublin, Wolfhound Press, 1981), p. 14.

Giesecke, H. (1999) Das 'Ende der Erziehung'. Ende oder Anfang pädagogischer Professionalität. *Pädagogische Professionalität*. A. Combe and W. Helsper. (Frankfurt: Main)

Grace, G., *Catholic Schools and the Common Good, What This Means in Educational Practice*, (London, Institute of Education, 21 September 2000).

Hargreaves, A., Goodson, I. (1996) 'Teachers Professional Lives: aspirations and actualities' in Goodson, I., Hargreaves, A., *Teachers; Professional Lives*, (London: Flamer Press).

Hay, D., Nye, R. (1998) *The Spirit of the Child*, (London: Fount).

Hogan, P. (1995) *The Custody and Courtship of Experience: Western Education in Philosophical Perspective*, (Dublin: Columba Press).

Hogan, P., 'Can Goodness be Taught?', in *The Furrow*, (Maynooth, February 1989).

Hogan, P., 'Schooling, Religious Tradition and the Default of God', in *The Furrow*, (Maynooth, July 1985).

Hogan, P., 'The Question of Ethos in Schools' in *The Furrow*, (November 1984).

Hogan, P., *The Custody and the Courtship of Experience*, (Dublin, Columba Press, 1995).

Inglis, T., *Moral Monopoly, The Rise and Fall of the Catholic Church in Modern Ireland*, (Dublin, Gill and Mac Millan, 1998).

INTO, *The Place of Religious Education in the National School System*, (Dublin, INTO, 1991).

Irish Bishops' Conference, *Developing a Policy for RSE in Catholic Schools*, (Maynooth, September, 1997).

Irish Bishops' Conference, *Education Bill 1997*, (Dublin, Catholic Communications Office, 12 March 1997).

Irish Bishops' Conference, *Guidelines for the Faith Formation and Development of Catholic Students*, (Dublin, Veritas, 1999).

John Paul II, *Catechesi Tradendae*, (Rome, 1979).

Jones, Jack, *In Your Opinion, Political and Social Trends in Ireland Through the Eyes of the Electorate*, (Dublin, Townhouse, 2001).

Kohlberg, L. (1981) *The Meaning and Measurement of Moral Development*, (London: Longman).

Lane, D., *Catholic Education and the School*, (Dublin, Veritas, 1991).

Lane, D., *Religion and Culture in Dialogue*, (Dublin, Columba Press, 1993).

Lang P., Katz, Y., Menezes, I.(1998) *Affective Education*, (London: Cassell).

Lang. P. (1983) 'Pastoral Care: Some reflections and Possible Influences' in *Pastoral Care in Education*, 2 (2).

Lynch, K., Lodge, A., *Equality in Education*, (Dublin, Gill and MacMillan, 1999).

Martin, M., *Discipline in Schools, Report to the Minister for Education, Niamh Breathnach*, (Dublin, Government Publications, 1997).

Maslow, A., *Towards a Psychology of Being*, (1968).

McCormack, T., 'Future Directions in Trusteeship', in Furlong, C., Monahan, L., *School Culture and Ethos, Cracking the Code*, (Dublin, Marino, 2000).

McDonnell, M. , *Ethos in Catholic Voluntary Secondary Schools*, (Dublin, UCD Unpublished Ph.D. Thesis, 1995).

McLoughlin, T., O'Keefe, J., O'Keefe, B., *The Contemporary Catholic School, Context, Identity and Diversity*, (London, Falmer Press, 1996).

Mulcahy, C., *Pluralism in Education, An Occasional Paper*, (Dublin, Centre for Pluralism in Education, DCU, 1998).

Murray, D., *A Special Concern, The Philosophy of Education: a Christian Perspective*, (Dublin, Veritas, 1991).

National Council for Curriculum Assessment, *Syllabus for Religious Education, Junior Certificate*, (May 1997).

National Education Convention 1993, *Presentation of Irish Bishops' Conference*, (Dublin, Government Publications, 1994).

National Education Convention 1993, *Presentation of the Conference of Religious in Ireland*, (Dublin, Government Publications, 1994).

Norman, J. (2002) *Pastoral Care in Second-Level Schools: The Chaplain* (Dublin: Centre for Research in Religion & Education).

Norman, J., 'Educational Underachievement: The Contribution of School Chaplaincy and Pastoral Care' in Educational Studies Vol. 21 (Dublin, ESAI, March 2002).

O'Donoghue, T., *The Catholic Church and the Secondary School Curriculum in Ireland 1922–1962*, (New York, Peter Lang, 1999).

O'Flaherty, L., *Management and Control in Irish Education*, (Dublin, Drumcondra Teacher's Centre, 1992).

O'Keefe, T., 'Values in a Christian School', in Feheney, *From Ideal to Action*, (Dublin, Veritas, 1998).

Parks, T. (2000) *An Italian Education* (London, Vintage).

Phinn, G., *Over Hill and Dale* (London, Penguin, 2000), p. 172.

Plato, Republic.

Report of the National Education Convention (1994) (Dublin: National Education Convention Secretariat).

Rodger, A. (1996) 'Human Spirituality: Towards an Educational Rationale' in Best . R., *Education, Spirituality and the Whole Child*, (London, Cassell, 1996).

Rogers, K. (1975) 'Empathic: an unappreciated way of being' in *The Counselling Psychologist*, Vol. 5(2) 2.

Rogers, K.(1969) *Freedom to Learn*, (Columbus, Ohio: Charles E. Merrill).

Sacred Congregation for Catholic Education (1998) *The Religious Dimension of Education in a Catholic School*, (Rome).

Sardar, Z. (200) 'Professionals who lost their virtue' in *New Statesman*, (10 July) pp. 25–7.

Second Vatican Council, *Declaration on Religious Liberty*, (Rome, 1965).

Smyth, A. (1996) *Discipline for Learning*, (Langford, 1996).

Smyth, E., *Do Schools Differ? Academic and Personal Development Among Pupils in the Second Level Sector*, (Dublin, Oak Tree Press & ESRI, 1999).

Sullivan, J., 'Compliance or Complaint: Some Difficulties Regarding Teachers in Catholic Schools' in *Irish Educational Studies*, Vol. 17.

Talbot, M. (2000) 'Developing SMSC for the Curriculum' in Best, R., *Education for Spiritual, Moral, Social and Cultural Development*, (London, Continuum).

Tuohy, D., Cairns, P. (2000) *Youth 2K: Threat or Promise to a Religious Culture'*, (Dublin: Marino).

White Paper on Education (1995), Charting Our Education Future, (Dublin, Government Publications, 1995).

Williams K., 'Understanding Ethos, A Philosophical and Literary Exploration' in Furlong, C., Monahan, L., *School Culture ad Ethos, Cracking the Code*, (Dublin, Marino, 2000).

Williams, K. (2001) 'Professions and Professionalism: The Case of Teaching' in *Issues in Education, ASTI Education Journal*, Vol. 4 (Dublin, Association of Secondary Teachers of Ireland).

Williams, K. 'Faith and the Nation: Education and Religious Identity in the Republic of Ireland', *British Journal of Educational Studies*, vol. 47. no. 4, (December, 1999), pp.317–31.

Williams, K. and McNamara, G., 'The Landscape of Curriculum Inquiry in Ireland', in W. Pinar, ed, *Handbook of International Curriculum Inquiry* (Mahwah, New Jersey, Lawrence Erlbaum, forthcoming).

Index

Irish Studies

Edited by Robert Mahony

The popularity of Irish Studies among both students and scholars has grown very markedly in the 1980s and 1990s, extending well beyond Ireland. This series is designed to serve and foster that interest. Currently featuring works in Irish history and literature, this interdisciplinary series will broaden its scholarly range in the future to include political and cultural studies generally.

For further information, or the submission of manuscripts, please contact:

Peter Lang Publishing
Acquisitions Department
275 7th Avenue, 28th Floor
New York, New York 10001

To order other books in this series, please contact our Customer Service Department:
(800) 770-LANG (within the U.S.)
(212) 647-7706 (outside the U.S.)
(212) 647-7707 FAX

Or browse online by series:
www.peterlangusa.com